PRACTICAL GRAMMAR

OF THE

ARABIC LANGUAGE.

WITH

INTERLINEAL READING LESSONS,

DIALOGUES AND VOCABULARY.

BY

FARIS EL-SHIDIAC

DARF PUBLISHERS LIMITED
LONDON
1988

New Impression 1988

ISBN 1 85077 187 1

Printed and bound in Great Britain
by A. Wheaton & Co. Ltd, Exeter, Devon

PREFACE.

———

In writing this Introduction to the Arabic Language
I, do not pretend to have performed a work of great
research; but I may justly state that I have produced a
most useful and practical work for those who wish to
study this Language, no such book having ever appeared
before in this country. As to the method of writing
Arabic words with English characters, it was made at
the suggestion of the publisher.

I have to thank the Rev. H. G. Williams, Professor
of Arabic at Cambridge, for many hints, especially for
correcting the English.

———

الحمد لله '

وبعد فاني لست ادّعي باني ابديت معجزة في تاليف هذا الكتاب
ولكن يحق لي ان اقول اني صنعت انفع شي لمن يروم ان يتعلم اللغة
العربية اذ لم يظهر الي الان كتاب مثله في لغة الانكليز اما كَتْب
الالفاظ العربية بحروف انكليزية فكان بحسب اشارة ناشره مستر كوارج ثم
ينبغي لي ان اثني علي الاب المحترم مستر وليامس مدرس اللغة العربية
في مدينة كمبريج وخصوصا علي تصليحه العبارات الانكليزية فلست والحالة
هذه اخجل من التنويه بهذا الكتاب علي صغر حجمه عند المبتدئين
رجاء ان ينوّه بي هو ايضا عند المنتهين *

A

GRAMMAR

OF THE

ARABIC LANGUAGE.

CHAPTER I.

THE Arabians, in common with many of the Eastern nations, write from the right hand to the left. Their Alphabet consists of twenty-eight letters, differently shaped according to their position at the beginning, middle, or end of words. The names and powers, and the order and figure, of the letters may be seen in the following Table.

ALPHABETICAL TABLE.

NAME.	FINAL.		MED.	INIT.	POWER.
	Connect.	Uncon.	Connect.		
Alif	ا	ا	ا	ا	a
Ba	ب	ب	ﺒ	ﺑ	b
Ta	ت	ت	ﺘ	ﺗ	t
Tha	ث	ث	ﺜ	ﺛ	th
Jeem	ج	ج	ﺠ	ﺟ	j
'Ha	ح	ح	ﺤ	ﺣ	h
C'ha	خ	خ	ﺨ	ﺧ	ch
Dal	د	د	ﺪ	ﺩ	d
Thal	ذ	ذ	ﺬ	ﺩ	th
Ra	ـر	ر	ـر	ر	r
Zaï or Zine ..	ـز	ز	ـز	ز	z
Seen	س	س	ﺴ	ﺳ	s
Sheen	ش	ش	ﺸ	ﺷ	sh
'Sad	ص	ص	ﺼ	ﺻ	s
'Dad	ض	ض	ﺾ	ﺿ	d
'Ta	ط	ط	ﻄ	ﻃ	t
Tha	ظ	ظ	ﻈ	ﻇ	th in *father*
Aine	ع	ع	ﻌ	ﻋ	a
Gine	غ	غ	ﻐ	ﻏ	g
Fa	ف	ف	ﻔ	ﻓ	f
'Kaf	ق	ق	ﻘ	ﻗ	k

NAME.	FINAL.		MED.	INIT.	POWER.
	Connect.	Uncon.	Connect.		
Kaf	كـ	ك	كـ	كـ	*k*
Lam........	ـل	ل	ـلـ	لـ	*l*
Meem	ـم	م	ـمـ	مـ	*m*
Noon........	ـن	ن	ـنـ	نـ	*n*
Waw........	ـو	و	ـو	و	*w*
Ha.........	ـه	ة	ـهـ	هـ	*h*
	،	ه	ـهـ		
Ya.........	ـي	ي	ـيـ	يـ	*y, i*

Lam-Alif, لا or لا, which is composed of ل *lam* and
ا *alif*.

OBSERVATIONS.

ث is pronounced like *th* in *thick*.

خ is a strong guttural.

ذ is equivalent to *th* in *this*.

ض. The *true* sound of this letter must be learnt by
the ear.   It is like a strong *d*.

ع resembles *Alif* with (ٔ) in sound, but is more
guttural.

غ is a hard guttural *g*.

ق is a guttural *k*.

CHAPTER II.

OF VOWELS AND ORTHOGRAPHICAL SIGNS.

The Arabs have only three characters for vowels, which they call فَتْحَة *Fatha*, كَسْرَة *Casra*, and ضَمَّة *Damma*. The first is represented by a small oblique line over the letter; the second by a similar stroke under the letter; and the third by a small curve, like a comma, as follows:

Fatha.. (َ) sounding as *a*.

Casra.. (ِ) sounding as *i*.

Damma (ُ) sounding nearly as *o*.

These signs are sometimes doubled in the final letters, which doubling is then called تَنْوِين *tanween*, or *nunation*, because the vowel is then pronounced as if terminated by ن, as رَجُلٌ *rajolon*, "a man;" رَجُلٍ *rajolin*; رَجُلاً *rajolan*. The first (ٌ) marks the nominative case; the second (ٍ) the genitive, dative, and ablative; the third (ً) the accusative. It must be observed here that the final ا adds nothing to the sound when the accusative is pronounced.

تَشْدِيد *tashdíd* (ّ) doubles the letter over which it is placed, as نَزَّلَ *nazzala*, "he brought down."

هَمْزَة *hamza* (ء) is placed generally over the ا, and sometimes over the و and ي, and is considered as a guttural letter.

وَصْل *wasla* (ٱ) implies *conjunction*, and is only inscribed over ا to mark an union with the preceding letter,

ا being then silent, as كِتَابُ ٱللّٰه *kitábu-lláhi*, "the book of God."

مَدَّة *madda* (~) implies *extension*, and is placed over ا, giving it a long sound, as آدَم *ádam*.

سكون *socoon* (°) signifies *a pause*, and is placed over a letter that has no vowel.

CHAPTER III.

OF THE NOUN.

THE Arabs consider the verb as the first part of speech, and the third person singular masculine of the preterite tense as the root or origin; but as the noun is more familiar to the English reader, we have placed it here before the verb. A few words, however, may be first said respecting the article ال, which the Arabs call أَدَاةُ ٱلتَّعْرِيف *adátuttaعríf*, "instrument of determination."

When any of these letters, namely, ت ث د ذ ر ز س ش ص ض ط ظ ن follows the article ال, the ل is then dropped, its place being supplied by *tashdíd*, as فِقْهُ ٱلدِّينِ *fikhu-ddín*, "knowledge of the religion."

When the particle ل *to* is prefixed to a noun beginning with ل, which, as being definite, ought to have the article, in order to avoid the meeting of several Lams the article is dispensed with; or, in pointed books, represented by *tashdíd*, as اِنّا لِلَّٰه *innâ lillâhi*, "we are to God."

N.B. The noun to which the article is annexed does not receive the tanween.

CHAPTER IV.

OF GENDER.

IN the Arabic there are two genders, مُذَكَّر *mothakkar*, "masculine," and مُؤَنَّث *moännath*, "feminine." Nouns are feminine either by signification or termination. By signification: 1st, names of women and female appellatives, as مَرْيَم *Mar-yam*, "Mary;" أُمّ *omm*, "a mother;" بِنْت *bint*, "a girl;" أُخْت *ocht*, "a sister:" 2dly, the double members of the body, as يَد *yad*, "the hand;" عَيْن *aine*, "the eye;" كَتِف *catif*, "the shoulder:" 3dly, names of countries and towns, as مِصْر *Misr*, "Egypt;" مَكَّة "Mecca."

By termination; 1st in ة, as جَنَّة *jannah*, "a garden;" ظُلْمَة *tholmah*, "darkness:" 2dly in ا servile, as بَيْضَا *bydâ*, "white:" 3dly in ي servile, pronounced like ا, as ذِكْرَى *thikra*, "remembrance;" أُولَى *oula*, "first." There are a few words which are to be learnt by practice and observation, being used feminine neither by signification nor by termination; such as أَرْض *ard*, "the earth;" خَمْر *chamr*, "wine;" حَرْب *karb*, "war;" نَار *nâr*, "fire;" رِيح *reah*, "the wind;" شَمْس *shams*, "the sun," &c. &c.

All other words are masculine.

Feminines are formed from masculines chiefly by the addition of ة, as طَيِّب *'ty-ib*, "good," طَيِّبة *'ty-ibah*; مَلِك *malik*, "a king," مَلِكة *malicah*, "a queen."

CHAPTER V.

OF NUMBER.

THERE are three numbers, singular, dual, and plural. The dual is formed by adding to the singular ان in the nominative case, and ين in the other cases. The plural is either perfect or imperfect. The perfect plural is that which ends in ون in the nominative case, and in ين in the other cases. The perfect feminines form their plural by adding ات. The imperfect plurals are such as are not formed by the addition of ون or ين, and are so extremely irregular and various, that no rules can greatly assist the memory.

FIRST DECLENSION, BEING TRIPTOTS, OR HAVING SINGULAR, DUAL, AND PLURAL.

SING.	DUAL.	PLURAL.
Nom. بَيْت a house.	بَيْتَان	بُيُوت
Gen. بَيْت	بَيْتَين	بُيُوت
Acc. بَيْتَا	. .	بُيُوتَا

SECOND DECLENSION, BEING PERFECT.

	SING.	DUAL.	PLURAL.
Nom.	كاتِبٌ writing.	كاتِبانِ	كاتِبُونَ
Gen.	كاتِبٍ	كاتِبَيْنِ	كاتِبِينَ
Acc.	كاتِبًا	..	..

THIRD DECLENSION FEMININE OF THE ABOVE.

Nom.	كاتِبَةٌ	كاتِبَتانِ	كاتِباتٌ
Gen.	كاتِبَةٍ	كاتِبَتَيْنِ	كاتِباتٍ
Acc.	كاتِبَةً	..	..

CHAPTER VI.

OF THE PRONOUN.

THE Arabs acknowledge only three parts of speech,
namely, the Verb, the Noun, and the Particle, including
under the noun the pronoun and the adjective.

The PERSONAL PRONOUNS are as follows:

	SING.		DUAL.	PLURAL.	
	M.	F.		M.	F.
First person....	أَنا	..	..	نَحْنُ	..
Second	أَنْتَ	أَنْتِ	أَنْتُما	أَنْتُم	أَنْتُنَّ
Third	هُوَ	هِيَ	هُما	هُم	هُنَّ

N.B. The dual and the plural feminine are not used in
the vulgar Arabic.

The DEMONSTRATIVE PRONOUNS are هَذَا "this," and ذَلِك "that," declined as follows:

	SING.	DUAL.	PLURAL.
Masc......	هَذَا	هَذَانِ هَذَينِ	هُوْلَآءِ
Fem.	هَذِهِ	هَتَانِ هَتَينِ	..

N.B. In the vulgar Arabic the singular only is used, and the plural is sometimes replaced by the word هَدُول, and at other times by هَدُونِ, or دُول, or هَدُولي, &c.

	SING.	DUAL.	PLURAL.
Masc......	ذَلِك	ذَانِك ذَينِك	أُولَائِك
Fem.	تِلْك	تَانِك تَينِك	..

THE RELATIVE PRONOUNS.

الَّذِي "who," is thus declined.

	SING.	DUAL.	PLURAL.
Masc......	الَّذِي	اللَّذانِ	الَّذِينِ
Fem.	الَّتِي	اللَّتانِ	اللَّاتِي

N.B. All these forms are replaced in the vulgar by the word الِّي.

مَنْ who, he who, those who, whoever.

ما that which, those which, whatever.

أَيّ who, which, what, of what kind.

THE POSSESSIVE PRONOUNS.

The possessive pronouns are expressed by means of affixes to the nouns; thus—

SING.		DUAL.	PLURAL.
كِتَابِي	my book.	..	كتابنا
كِتَابُكَ	thy (*m*) book.	كتابُكما	كتابُكم
كِتَابُكِ	thy (*f*) book.		كتابُكن
كِتَابُه	his book.	كِتابُهما	كتابُهم
كِتَابُها	her book.		كتابُهن

The dual, and also the plural feminine, are not commonly used.

The same affixes are used with prepositions: for instance,

SING.		DUAL.	PLURAL.
مِنِّي	from me.	..	منّا
مِنْكَ	from thee (*m*).	منكُما	منكم
مِنْكِ	from thee (*f*).		منكن
مِنْه	from him.	منهُما	منهُم
مِنْها	from her.		منهن

N.B. The same affixes serve as the accusative cases after verbs.

CHAPTER VII.

OF COMPARISON.

THE comparative is formed from the positive of the triliteral verb, upon the measure of أَفْعَل; as, كَبِيْر "great," أَكْبَر "greater;" جَمِيْل "beautiful," أَجْمَل "more beautiful."

CHAPTER VIII.

OF THE NOUN OF PLACE AND TIME.

THE same form of noun is used to denote time and place, and is regularly derived from the triliteral verb upon the measure مَفْعَل; as, مَكْتَب "time or place of writing;" مَلْعَب "time or place of playing;" مَقْعَد "time or place of sitting." Or upon the measure مَفْعِل; as, مَضْرِب "time or place of beating."

CHAPTER IX.

OF THE NOUN DENOTING THE INSTRUMENT.

THE noun denoting the instrument is derived from the triliteral verb, and has three forms: 1. مِفْعَل; as, مِبْرَد "a file." 2. مِفْعَال; as, مِفْتَاح "a key." 3. مِفْعَلَة; as, مِكْنَسَة "a broom."

GOAL—B

CHAPTER X.

OF THE NOUN DENOTING A SINGLE ACTION.

THIS noun has the measure of فَعْلَة; as, ضَرْبَة "once striking;" كَتْبَة "once writing," &c. &c.

N.B. All these forms are regularly derived from the verb which has three letters.

CHAPTER XI.

OF THE ADJECTIVES.

THERE are many forms in Arabic for the adjective: the most common are فَعِيْل; as, كَرِيْم "generous;" جَمِيْل "handsome;" and فَعُول; as, شَكُوْر "thankful;" صَبُوْر "patient."

There are also the forms فَعَّال and فَعِيل, denoting frequency or intensity; as, ضَرَّاب "one who strikes often," سِكِّيْر "very drunken:" فَعَل; as, حَسَن "beautiful:" as, فَرِح "glad, or merry:" فَعْلَان; as, عَطْشَان "thirsty."

The Arabic language, rich as it is in words and in modes of expression, has only one form of adjectives derived from substantives. It is formed by adding ي with (ّ) to the substantive; as, for instance, وَرْدِيّ "rosy;" مَآءِيّ "watery;" شَمْسِيّ "solar;" ارضِيّ "earthen," &c. &c. This ي is called يَآ النسب.

CHAPTER XII.

OF THE DIMINUTIVE.

THE diminutive is formed in general by inserting ـ after the second letter of the primitive; as, عُبَيْد "a little servant," from عَبْد "a servant;" رُجَيْل "a little man."

This form, although very convenient, yet is very seldom used, even in books.

CHAPTER XIII.

OF THE VERB.

THE Arabic verb, in its several conjugations, consists of three letters or more, up to six. The triliteral verb is divided into seven classes, named by the Arabs as follows, the names being derived from the circumstance of the verb having a letter doubled, or containing one of the letters, ا, و, or ي. In treating of the verbs, as well as in the other parts of the grammar, the different forms of the verb فَعَل "he did," are referred to as models. On this principle, the first radical letter of the verb is called the Fa, the second the Aine, the third the Lam.

1.... السالم, as كَتَب he wrote.

2.... المضاعف .. مَدَّ he stretched.

3.... المهموز .. أَخَذَ he took.

4.... المعتلّ الفآ .. وَعَدَ he promised.

5....المعتلّ العين, as   قَالَ   he said.

6.... المعتلّ اللام   ..   رَمَى   he threw.

7....   اللّفِيْف   ..   وَقَى   he preserved.

The verbs are either *triliteral* or *quadriliteral*; the first consisting of three radical letters, as those already instanced; the other of four, as دَحْرَج "he rolled."

The derivatives are divided into three classes; the first being augmented by one servile letter, the second by two, and the last by three, as in the following manner:

1......... فَعّل	6........ تَفَاعَل
2......... أَفْعل	7.... ... انْفَعل
3......... فَعّل	8........ افْتَعل
4......... فَاعل	9........ افْعَلّ
٥......... تَفعّل	10....... اسْتَفعل

The first conjugation has a transitive sense, where the action has an effect upon some other object, as كَتَبَ كتابًا "he wrote a book," and it is called مُتَعَدّي; and also an intransitive one, where the effect is confined within the agent, as حَزِن "he mourned," and it is called لازِم.

The second and third form transitives, as نَزّل or أَنْزل "he brought down," or, "he caused to go down;" with this difference, that the (ّ) indicates the action to have been done gradually, and the ا gives the idea that the action was done at once. But if the verb is originally transitive, the (˜) then gives it an intensive sense, as كَسَّرَ "he broke to pieces;" or it makes it transitive in two degrees, as كَتَّبَ "he caused somebody to write."

The fourth conveys the idea of a reciprocal action, as ضَارَبَ زَيدٌ عَمْرًا "Zeid beat Amr," implying, at the same time, that Amr beat Zeid in return; also an intransitive sense, as جَالَسَ زَيدٌ عَمْرًا "Zeid sat down with Amr."

The fifth has sometimes a passive signification, as تَكَسَّرَ "it was broken," being the passive of the second conjugation كَسَّرَ; and sometimes an active sense, as تَرَقَّبَ "he expected."

The sixth denotes a co-operation or mutual action, nearly corresponding with the fourth, as تَضَارَبَ القَوْمُ "the people beat each other."

The seventh denotes a passive sense, as اِنْكَسَرَ "it was broken."

The eighth has sometimes a passive sense, as اِجْتَمَعَ "it was collected;" and sometimes an active one, as اِخْتَرَعَ "he invented." The reason appears to be insufficient why most of the grammarians take it to be always passive.

The ninth form denotes colour, as اِصْفَرَّ "it became yellow;" it implies also deformity, as اِعْوَرَّ "he became one-eyed."

The tenth has generally two significations: the first is petitioning and desiring, as اِسْتَغْفَرَ "he asked pardon;" the second implies considering the thing to be such as is ex-

pressed by the simple verb, *e. g.* اِسْتَحْسَنَ "he considered
(it) to be pretty;" اِسْتَغْلَى "he considered (it) to be dear."

The Arabs arrange their moods and tenses differently
from the Europeans, dividing their conjugation into five
parts: 1st, the Preterite; 2d, the Future; 3d, the Imperative; 4th, the Participle; and 5th, the Infinitive.

Excepting the infinitive, they all have three numbers—
singular, dual, and plural; and two genders—masculine
and feminine. Their persons, as in other languages, are
three; but the third being the root, precedes the second,
and the second the first; all which will appear sufficiently
obvious from the following paradigms:

CONJUGATION OF THE FIRST FORM OF REGULAR TRILITERAL VERBS.

ACTIVE VOICE.

Preterite.

PLURAL.		DUAL.		SING.		
F.	M.	F.	M.	F.	M.	
نَصَرْنَ	نَصَرُوا	نَصَرَتَا	نَصَرَا	نَصَرَتْ	نَصَرَ	3
نَصَرْتُنَّ	نَصَرْتُمْ	نَصَرْتُمَا		نَصَرْتِ	نَصَرْتَ	2
نَصَرْنَا		..		نَصَرْتُ		1

Present or Future.

يَنْصُرْنَ	يَنْصُرُونَ	تَنْصُرَانِ	يَنْصُرَانِ	تَنْصُرُ	يَنْصُرُ	3
تَنْصُرْنَ	تَنْصُرُونَ	تَنْصُرَانِ		تَنْصُرِينَ	تَنْصُرُ	2
نَنْصُرُ		..		أَنْصُرُ		1

OF THE VERB.

17

Imperative.

PLURAL.		DUAL.		SING.	
F.	M.	F.	M.	F.	M.
اُنصُرنَ	اُنصُروا		اُنصُرا	اُنصُري	اُنصُر

Participle.

PLURAL.		DUAL.		SING.	
ناصِراتٌ	ناصِرونَ	ناصِرتانِ	ناصِرانِ	ناصِرةٌ	ناصِرٌ

Infinitive.

نَصرٌ

PASSIVE VOICE.

The passive voice differs from the active chiefly in the vowel points, as may be observed by comparing them together.

Preterite.

PLURAL.		DUAL.		SING.		
F.	M.	F.	M.	F.	M.	
نُصِرنَ	نُصِروا	نُصِرتا	نُصِرا	نُصِرت	نُصِر	3
نُصِرتِن	نُصِرتم		نُصِرتُما	نُصِرت	نُصِرت	2
	نُصِرنا		..		نُصِرت	1

Future.

PLURAL.		DUAL.		SING.		
ينصَرن	ينصَرون	تنصَرانِ	ينصَرانِ	تنصَر	ينصَر	3
تنصَرن	تنصَرون		تنصَرانِ	تنصَرين	تنصَر	2
	ننصَر		..		أنصَر	1

C

Participle.

PLURAL.		DUAL.		SING.	
F.	M.	F.	M.	F.	M.
منصورات	منصورون	منصورتانِ	منصورانِ	منصورة	منصور

The imperative passive is formed from the future by adding ا to it, as لِينصرْ, لانصرْ, لِننصرْ.

CHAPTER XIV.

IT is requisite, in place of swelling the grammar unnecessarily with a great number of whole-length conjugations, to give the first word alone of every tense, leaving it to the learner, by way of exercise, to fill up the other persons, which he may find to be a considerable help to his memory.

OF THE DERIVATIVE THREE-LETTER CONJUGATION.

ACTIVE VOICE.

First Class.

PART.	IMPER.	INFIN.	FUTURE.	PRET.
مفعِل	افعِلْ	افعالًا	يفعِل	افعَل
مفعِّل	فعِّل	تفعيلًا	يفعِّل	فعَّل
مفاعِل	فاعِلْ	مفاعلةً وفِعالًا	يفاعِل	فاعَل

Second Class.

PART.	IMPER.	INFIN.	FUTURE.	PRET.
مُتَفَعِّل	تَفَعَّلْ	تَفَعُّلاً	يَتَفَعَّلُ	تَفَعَّلَ
مُتَفَاعِل	تَفَاعَلْ	تَفَاعُلاً	يَتَفَاعَلُ	تَفَاعَلَ
مُنْفَعِل	اِنْفَعِلْ	اِنْفِعَالاً	يَنْفَعِلُ	اِنْفَعَلَ
مُفْتَعِل	اِفْتَعِلْ	اِفْتِعَالاً	يَفْتَعِلُ	اِفْتَعَلَ
مُفْعِل	اِفْعَلِلْ	اِفْعِلالاً	يَفْعَلُّ	اِفْعَلَّ

Third Class.

مُسْتَفْعِل	اِسْتَفْعِلْ	اِسْتِفْعَالاً	يَسْتَفْعِلُ	اِسْتَفْعَلَ

OBSERVATIONS.

The infinitive of the triliteral verb is irregular. The dual forms and the feminine plurals are not used in common conversation.

CONJUGATION OF THE VERB مضاعف (DOUBLED).

Preterite.

PLURAL.		DUAL.		SING.	
F.	M.	F.	M.	F.	M.
مَدَدْنَ	مَدُّوا	مَدَّتَا	مَدَّا	مَدَّتْ	مَدَّ
مَدَدْتُنَّ	مَدَدْتُمْ	مَدَدْتُمَا		مَدَدْتِ	مَدَدْتَ
مَدَدْنَا		..		مَدَدْتُ	

c 2

OF THE VERB.

Future.

PLURAL.		DUAL.		SING.	
F.	M.	F.	M.	F.	M.
يَمْدُدْنَ	يَمُدُّونَ	تَمُدَّانِ	يَمُدَّانِ	تَمُدُّ	يَمُدُّ
تَمْدُدْنَ	تَمُدُّونَ	تَمُدَّانِ		تَمُدِّينَ	تَمُدُّ
نَمُدُّ		..		أَمُدُّ	

Imperative.

أُمْدُدْنَ	مُدُّوا	مُدَّا	مُدِّي	مُدَّ

Participle.

مَادَّاتٌ	مَادُّونَ	مَادَّتَانِ	مَادَّانِ	مَادَّةٌ	مَادٌّ

Passive.

PART.	FUT.	PRET.
مَمْدُودٌ	يُمَدُّ	مُدَّ

CONJUGATION OF THE VERB معتل الفآء (*lit.* " WEAK OF THE FA," HAVING THE FIRST RADICAL و).

Preterite.

PLURAL.		DUAL.		SING.	
F.	M.	F.	M.	F.	M.
وَعَدْنَ	وَعَدُوا	وَعَدَتَا	وَعَدَا	وَعَدَتْ	وَعَدَ
وَعَدْتُنَّ	وَعَدْتُمْ	وَعَدْتُمَا		وَعَدْتِ	وَعَدْتَ
وَعَدْنَا		..		وَعَدْتُ	

Future.

PLURAL.		DUAL.		SING.	
F.	M.	F.	M.	F.	M.
يَعِدْنَ	يَعِدُونَ	تَعِدانِ	يَعِدانِ	تَعِدُ	يَعِدُ
تَعِدْنَ	تَعِدُونَ		تَعِدانِ	تَعِدِينَ	تَعِدُ
	نَعِدُ		..		أَعِدُ

Imperative.

عِدْنَ	عِدُوا	عِدا	عِدِي	عِدْ

Participle.

واعِداتٌ	واعِدُونَ	واعِدَتانِ	واعِدانِ	واعِدَةٌ	واعِدٌ

CONJUGATION OF THE VERB معتل العين (*lit.* "WEAK OF
THE AINE," HAVING THE SECOND RADICAL و).

Preterite.

PLURAL.		DUAL.		SING.	
F.	M.	F.	M.	F.	M.
قُلْنَ	قالُوا	قالَتا	قالا	قالَتْ	قالَ
قُلْتُنَّ	قُلْتُمْ	قُلْتُما		قُلْتِ	قُلْتَ
	قُلْنا		..		قُلْتُ

Future.

PLURAL.		DUAL.		SING.	
يَقُلْنَ	يَقُولُونَ	تَقُولانِ	يَقُولانِ	تَقُولُ	يَقُولُ
تَقُلْنَ	تَقُولُونَ		تَقُولانِ	تَقُولِينَ	تَقُولُ
	نَقُولُ		..		أَقُولُ

Imperative.

PLURAL.		DUAL.		SING.	
F.	M.	F.	M.	F.	M.
قُلْنَ	قُولُوا		قُولَا	قُولِي	قُلْ

Participle.

قَائِلَاتٌ	قَائِلُونَ	قَائِلَتَانِ	قَائِلَانِ	قَائِلَةٌ	قَائِلٌ

Passive.

PART.	FUT.	PRET.
مَقُولٌ	يُقَالُ	قِيلَ

CONJUGATION OF THE VERB مُعْتَلُّ اللَّامِ (*lit.* "WEAK OF THE LAM," HAVING THE THIRD RADICAL ي).

Preterite.

PLURAL.		DUAL.		SING.	
F.	M.	F.	M.	F.	M.
رَمَيْنَ	رَمَوْا	رَمَتَا	رَمَيَا	رَمَتْ	رَمَى
رَمَيْتُنَّ	رَمَيْتُمْ		رَمَيْتُمَا	رَمَيْتِ	رَمَيْتَ
	رَمَيْنَا				رَمَيْتُ

Future.

PLURAL.		DUAL.		SING.	
يَرْمِينَ	يَرْمُونَ	يَرْمِيَانِ	يَرْمِيَانِ	تَرْمِي	يَرْمِي
تَرْمِينَ	تَرْمُونَ	تَرْمِيَانِ	تَرْمِيَانِ	تَرْمِينَ	تَرْمِي
	نَرْمِي				أَرْمِي

Imperative.

PLURAL.		DUAL.		SING.	
F.	M.	F.	M.	F.	M.
اِرْمِينَ	اِرْمُوا	اِرْمِيا		اِرْمِي	اِرْمِ

Participle.

رَامِيَاتٌ	رَامُونَ	رَامِيَتَانِ	رَامِيَانِ	رَامِيَةٌ	رَامٍ

Passive.

PART.	FUT.	PRET.
مرْمِيّ	يرمي	رُمِيَ

CHAPTER XV.

OF PREPOSITIONS.

THE prepositions in Arabic require the genitive case after them. They are called حُرُوفُ الْجَرِّ, *particles of attraction;* and the word which follows them is said to be مَجْرُور, and is marked with a *casra, e.g.* مِنْ رَجُلٍ "from a man;" مِنَ الرَّجُلِ "from the man." The following is a list of the prepositions:

   بِ   by, in.

   تَ   by (only in conjuring).

و		by (only in conjuring).
لِ		to, for.
كَ		like, as.

These five particles are prefixed to the words they govern.

مِن	min,	from.
الى	ila,	to.
عن	ɛan,	of, from.
على	ɛala,	upon.
فى	fi,	in.
رب	robba,	it may be.
مذ	moth,	since.
منذ	month,	since.
حاشا	'hâsha,	except.
عدا	ɛada,	except.
خلا	ćhala,	except.
حتى	'hatta,	even to.

The following words, most of which have the force of prepositions, also require the genitive case after them.

كلّ	coll,	every, all.
مع	maɛ,	with.
جيع	jamiɛ,	all, altogether.
بعد	baɛd,	after.
قبل	'kabl,	before.
فوق	fou'k,	above, over.

تحت	*ta'ht,*	under.
قدّام	*'koddâm,*	before.
ورآ	*warā,*	behind.
مثل	*mithl,*	like.
شبه	*shibh,*	like.
نظير	*nathir,*	like.
نحو	*na'how,*	about, like.
عند	*ꭼind,*	at, with.
سوي	*siwa,*	except, besides.
غير	*ghire,*	except, besides.
حذآ	*'hithâ,*	by, by side of.
قالة	*'kobâlah,*	opposite.
ازآ	*izâ,*	near, by.
تجاه	*tujâh,*	opposite.
تلقا	*til'kâ,*	opposite.
ذو	*thoo,*	having, possessing.
لدي	*lada,*	at.
لدن	*ladon,*	at.
وسط	*wasa't,*	in the middle of.

CHAPTER XVI.

OF CONJUNCTIONS.

The following are the conjunctions in most common use:

وَ "and."—Ex. جآ زَيد وَعَمْرو " Zeid *and* Amr came."

فَ "and."—Ex. قَرَأْتُ الصَّرْفَ فَالنَّحْوَ "I have read etymology *and* syntax. The particle وَ is irrespective of order : فَ, on the contrary, distinguishes it. I have read etymology *first*, and *then* syntax.

ثم *thumma*, "then."—Ex. جَاءَ الرِّجَالُ ثُمَّ النِّسَآءَ "The men came, *then* the women."

حتي *'hatta*, "even."—Ex. أَكَلْتُ السَّمَكَةَ حَتَّي رَأْسَها "I have eaten the fish, *even* its head."

او *au*, "or."—Ex. إِلْبَسِ الصَّوْفَ أَوِ الحَرِيرَ "Be dressed in wool *or* silk."

ام *am*, "or."—Ex. أَزَيْدٌ قَامَ أَمْ عَمْرٌو "Did Zeid stand up, *or* Amr?"

ولا *walâ*, "and not," "nor."—Ex. مَا جَآءَنِي رَجُلٌ وَلا امْرَأَةٌ "A man did not come to me, *nor* a woman."

بل *bal*, "but."—Ex. مَا جَآءَنِي رَجُلٌ بَلِ امْرَأَةٌ "A man did not come to me, *but* a woman."

لكن *lâkin*, "but."—Ex. مَا رَأَيْتُ رَجُلًا لَكِنِ امْرَأَةً "I did not see a man, *but* a woman."

The following words and particles, many of which are

nouns in the accusative case, though used adverbially, will be of considerable use to the learner:

اتتدآءً	*ibtidâ-an,*	In the first place.
ابدًا	*abadan,*	never, for ever.
احتياطًا	*i'htiya'tan,*	cautiously.
أَحْيانًا	*a'hyânan,*	sometimes.
اخيرًا	*âchiran,*	lastly.
آخر الامر	*âchira'l amr,*	at length.
اذ	*ith,*	when.
اذ ذاك	*ith thâk,*	then, at this time.
اذا	*ithâ,*	if, when, behold.
اذما	*ith ma,*	when.
اذن or اذاً	*ithan,*	then.
ارتجالاً	*irtijâlan,*	extempore.
اسفل	*asfal,*	below.
اصلًا	*aslan,*	never, not at all.
اضطرارًا	*id'tirâran,*	by force.
الآن	*al-ân,*	now.
الّا	*illâ,*	but, except.
الّا ان	*illâ an,*	unless.
اليوم	*al youm,*	to-day.
الى	*ila,*	to, until.
الى حيث	*ila 'hithe,*	whither.
الى غير ذلك	*ila ghire thâlik,*	et cætera.
الى الآن	*ila al-ân,*	hitherto.
الى هنا	*ila huna,*	hither.

اِمّا	immâ,	either.
اَمّا	ammâ,	but, as to.
امام	amâm,	before.
ان	an,	that (before a verb).
اِنّ	inna,	certainly.
اَنّ	anna,	that (before a noun).
اِنّما	innamâ,	but, only.
او	au,	or.
اَوّلاً	awwalan,	at first.
اَوَلِم	awa lam,	is it not?
اهلاً	ahlan,	welcome.
اَيْ	eye,	that is, viz.
اَيّ	eyee,	which of.
اِيّاك	iyâk,	take you care.
اِيضاً	eyedan,	also.
اَين	eyen, aine,	where?
باطلا	bâ'tilan,	in vain.
بالحقّ	bil'ha'k'k,	justly.
البتّة or بتة	albattah,	not at all.
بدلاً من	badalan min,	instead of.
بديها	badihan,	extempore.
بَرّا	barra,	without.
بَعْد	baᶜd,	after.
وبعد	wa-baᶜdo,	and now.
بعد هذا	baᶜda-hâtha,	after this.
بعد غد	baᶜda gad	after to-morrow.

بَعيد	*ba𐤏id,*	far off.
من غير * بغير	*bighire, min ghire,*	without.
بكرة * باكرا	*bokrah,*	early.
بينما * بَيْنَ	*bine, bînamâ,*	between.
ثُمَّ	*thomma,*	and, then, therefore.
ثَمَّ	*thamma,*	there, in that place.
جبرًا	*jabran,*	by force.
جدًّا	*jiddan,*	very, in earnest.
جزمًا	*jazman,*	resolutely.
في الجملة * جُمْلَةً	*fi 'ljomlah,*	{ totally, upon the whole.
جميعًا	*jamî𐤏an,*	altogether.
حاشا	*'hâsha,*	except, God forbid.
حالًا	*'hâlan,*	presently.
حتّي	*'hatta,*	{ so that, in order to, until, even.
حتي اِنَّ	*'hatta inna,*	so that.
حتّي اذا	*hatta itha,*	until, when.
حتّيم	*'hatta ma,*	how long?
حِذآ	*'hithâ,*	over against.
حسب	*hasab,*	according to.
حقًا	*'ha'k'kan,*	certainly.
حَوْل	*'houle,*	around.

حَيْث	'haithe,	where.
حَيْثُما	'haithoma,	wherever.
حِينئذ	'hina-ithin,	then.
في الخارج or خارجا	c'harijan, fi 'lchârij,	without.
خصوصا * خاصة	ćhaśśah, ćhośoośan,	especially, peculiarly.
ماخلا * خلا	ćhala, mâ ćhala,	besides, except.
خَلْف	ćhalf,	behind.
دائما	dâ-iman,	at all times.
دون	doon,	under, besides.
من دون	min doon,	without.
رَبّما * رُبّ	robba, robbama,	there may be, perhaps, often.
رُوَيْداً	rowaidan,	softly, slowly.
سابقا	sâbi'kan,	formerly.
سابقًا ولاحقًا	sâbi'kan wa-lâ'hi'kan,	before and after.
سريعًا	sariɛan,	quickly.
سمعًا وطاعة	samɛan wa-'tâɛah,	obediently.
سَوْف	soufa,	after (connected with the verb).
شرعًا	sharɛan,	legally.
علي طِبْق * طِبْق	'tib'k, ɛala 'tib'k,	according, agreeing with.

طورًا	'touran,	once.
عاجلا	ᶜâjilan,	hastily.
ماعدا * عدا	ᶜada, ma ᶜada,	except.
لعلَّ * عَلَّ	ᶜalla, laᶜalla,	{ perhaps, I hope, by chance.
علي	ᶜala,	{ upon, above, against.
علي الخصوص	ᶜala 'lc'hóśoos,	particularly.
علي الدوام	ᶜala 'ddawâm,	always, continually.
علي الفور	ᶜala 'lfour,	quickly.
علي كل حال	ᶜala colli 'hâl,	{ on every state, in every manner.
علي اىّ حال	ᶜala eyei 'hâl,	
علي جدةٍ	ᶜala 'hidah,	alone, separately.
عن	ᶜan,	of, from, concerning
(عن ما) عمّا	ᶜamma,	of that which.
عند	ᶜind,	with, at.
عن قصد	ᶜan 'kaśd,	intentionally.
عن قريب	ᶜan 'karîb,	in a short time.
غالبًا	gâliban,	generally.
غِبّ	ghibb,	after.
غبّا	ghibban,	alternately.
غدا	gada,	to-morrow.
غير	ghire,	not.

غيراَنْ	ghira an,	except that.
من غير	min ghire,	} without.
بغير	bighire,	
غير بعيد	ghire baᶜîd,	not far.
ف	fa,	} and, then, therefore, &c.
فاِنَّ	fa-inna,	for, because.
فردا	fardan,	single.
فقط	fa'ka't,	only.
فوق	fou'k,	above.
فوق الحد	fou'k al'hadd,	above limit.
فوق القياس	fou'k al'kiyâs,	above measure.
في	fi,	in, into, among.
في اثناَ ذلك	fi athnâ thâlik,	} in the mean time.
في غضون ذلك	fi go'loon thâlik,	
في الجملة	fi 'ljomlah,	upon the whole.
في الحال	fi 'l'hâl,	immediately.
في الحقيقة	fi 'l'ha'hi'kah,	truly, in fact.
في الواقع	fi 'lwâkiᶜ,	in fact, really.
في كل مكان	fi colli macân,	in every place.
فيمَ	fîma,	in what? why?
من قبل * قبل	kabl, min 'kabl,	before.
فيما بعد	fimâ baᶜd,	henceforward.

فيما بعد	fîmâ baعd,	hereafter.
قبل الان	'kabl alân,	before now.
قد	'kad,	certainly.
قدام	'koddâm,	before.
قريب	'karîb,	near.
قط	'ka'tt,	never.
قطعا	'ka't عan,	never, in no shape.
قليلا	'kalîlan,	little.
كأنَّ	caanna,	as if.
كثيرًا ما	kathîran mâ,	often.
كذا	cathâ,	so, thus.
كذلك	kathâlik,	likewise.
كلّا	callâ,	not at all.
كل واحد * كل احد	coll a'had, coll wâ'hid,	every one.
كلّما	collamâ,	{ as often as, when-ever.
كل يوم	coll youm,	every day.
كم	cam,	{ how many, how much.
كما	camâ,	as.
لكي * كي	caye, likaye,	in order to.
كيف	kife,	how.
كيفما	'kîfamâ,	any how.

D

كيلا	keyelâ,	so as not.
كيما	keyemâ,	that.
ل	li,	to, for.
لا	la,	no, not.
لابُدّ	la bodd,	necessarily.
من اجل * لاجل	li-ajl, min ajl,	{ on which account, for.
لاشي	lâ shy,	nothing.
لا محالة	lâ ma'hâlah,	undoubtedly.
لِاَنَّ	li-anna,	because.
لِاَنْ	li-an,	that.
لَـبَّـيْـك	labbike,	here I am !
لدُن * لَدَي	lada, ladon,	at.
لكن	lâkin,	but.
لم	lam,	not.
لَمَّا	lamma,	not yet, when.
لماذا	li-mâthâ,	why.
لو	loue,	if.
لولِم * لولا	loue la, loue lam,	unless.
لَيْت	lite,	would to God.
ليس	lise,	no, not.
لثَلّا	li-alla,	that not.
ما	ma,	no, what, that which

ماين	ma bine,	between.
مادام	ma dâm,	as long as.
متي	mata,	when, whenever.
مِثْل	mithl,	like, as.
مدي الايام	mada'l ayyâm,	at all times.
مرحبا	mar'haba, marhaban,	welcome!
مرّة	marrah,	once.
مع	maع	with.
معًا	maعan,	together, along with
مفصّلا	mofaśsalan,	distinctly.
ممّا	mimmâ,	from that which.
ممّن	mimman,	from him who.
مَن	man,	who.
مِن	min,	from.
من الان	min alân,	from this time.
من الان فصاعدا	min alân faśâعidan,	henceforth.
من اين	min eyine,	whence.
من بعد	min baعd,	after.
من تحت	min ta'ht,	from below.
من حيث	min 'hithe,	since.
من دون	min doon,	⎫
من غير	min ghire,	⎬ without.
من فوق	min fou'k,	from above.

D 2

من هنا	*min honâ,*	} hence.
من هناك	*min honâk,*	
مهما	*mahmâ,*	as often as.
نحو	*na'hou,*	near about, as.
نعم	*naعam,*	yes.
و	*wa,*	and.
ورآ	*warâ,*	behind.
ولا	*walâ,*	neither.
ولو	*waloue,*	although.
ويل	*wile,*	fie,
ها	*hâ,*	behold.
هل	*hal,*	whether?
هنا	*honâ,*	here.
هنالك * هناك	*honâk, honâlik,*	there.
هوذا	*howa-thâ,*	behold.
يعني	*yaعni,*	that is to say.

CHAPTER XVII.
OF THE NUMERALS.

The Cardinal Numbers are the following :

	MASC.	FEM.		MASC.	FEM.
1.	واحِد / أحَد	واحِدَة / إِحْدَى	11.	أحد عشر	إحْدَى عشرة
2.	اِثْنان	اِثْنَتان	20.	عِشْرون	
3.	ثَلَاثَة	ثَلَاث	30.	ثَلَثُون	
4.	أربعة	أربع	40.	أربعون	
5.	خمسة	خمس	50.	خمسون	
6.	سِتَّة	سِت	. . . .		
7.	سبعة	سبع	100.	مائة	
8.	ثمانية	ثمان	200.	مائتان	
9.	تسعة	تسع	1000.	ألف	
10.	عشرة	عشر	2000.	ألفان	

The Ordinals are as follow :

	MASC.	FEM.		MASC.	FEM.
1st.	أوّل	أوْلَى	10th.	عاشِر	عاشِرة
2d.	ثانٍ	ثانِية	11th.	حادِي عشر	حادية عشرة
3d.	ثالث	ثالثة	. . . .		
4th.	رابع	رابعة	20th.	عِشْرون	
. . . .			30th.	ثَلَثُون &c.	

CHAPTER XVIII.

GENERAL OBSERVATIONS.

THE verbs in which one of the three letters, viz. ا و ي
occurs, present the greatest difficulties to the Arabic
student, as they are sometimes changed one for the other,
or dropped altogether. A little practice and observation
will, however, put the learner in possession of these irregu-
larities better than any rules with which to burden his
memory.

The form for the future of the verb is also applicable
for the present. The modern Arabs, therefore, make it a
real present by joining to it some other word. Thus
هُوَ يَكْتُب signifies *he writes,* or, *he will write.* But
هو عَمّال يكتب has the single signification of *he is writing.*

The words بدّه , بدّي , &c. placed before a verb, add to it
the signification of *is going.*—Ex. هو بدّه يخرج " he is going
to go out."

Although in the classical Arabic there are two particles, سَ and سوف , employed to confine the verb to the
future signification, they are very seldom used in ordinary
books.

The pluperfect in Arabic is expressed by the addition
of the verb كان " to be," to the principal verb."

Ex. كان كتب " he had written."

The most difficult point connected with nouns is the

imperfect plural, which is not formed by the addition of
ون or ات. It is so extremely irregular and various that
no rules can greatly assist the memory; but those forms
which most generally occur will soon become familiar,
and a dictionary will afford every necessary assistance
with regard to the more uncommon.

The principal forms, however, are comprehended in the
following table:

SING.		PLURAL.
غُرْفَة	a parlour	غُرَف
جِدار	a wall..........	جُدُر
أَحْمَر	red	حُمْر
قِرْبَة	a bladder	قِرَب
رِجُل	a man	رِجال
بَيْت	a house	بُيوت
ضارِب	striking	ضُرَّب
كامِل	perfect	كَمَلَة
رامٍ	throwing	رُماة
قِرْد	an ape	قِرَدَة
غُصْن	a branch	أَغْصان
جَبَل	a mountain......	أَجْبال
خاتَم	a seal	خَواتِم

SING.		PLURAL.
غُلَام	a boy	غِلْمَان
شَرِيف	noble	شُرَفَآء
جريح	wounded	جَرْحَي

With regard to the quadriliteral nouns, all the simple ones, and many of those which are augmented, together with their feminines, form their plurals by inserting ١ after the second letter, the first having (´), and the third (ِ), as كواكب, from كَوْكَب "a star;" دراهم, from دِرْهَم "a derham;" معابد, from مَعْبَد "a worshipping place," &c.

The modern Arabs use no particle for an interrogation, but denote it by the tone of voice. They sometimes, however, employ ش (which is a corruption of شي *shy*, "a thing") both in interrogative and negative sentences. Thus, they say, رحت ش اليوم عنده *ro'htish al-youm ʒindoh*, "Did you go to him to-day?" Also, ما رحت ش اليوم عنده *mâ ro'htish al-youm ʒindoh*, "I did not go to him to-day."

BOOK II.

SYNTAX.

CHAPTER I.

OF THE NOMINATIVE CASE OF THE NOUN.

THE *nominative* case is principally employed to express
the following:

1. المُبْتَدَا the subject.

2.   الخَبَر the predicate.

Ex. زَيدٌ كاتبٌ " *Zeid* (is) *writing;*" where زَيدٌ is the
subject, and كاتبٌ the predicate.

3. الفاعل the agent, as ضَرَبَ زَيدٌ " *Zeid* beat."

4. نائب الفاعل the substitute of the agent—the subject
of a passive verb.—Ex. ضُرِبَ زَيدٌ " *Zeid* was beaten."

5. المُنَادَي the *vocative,* as يا زَيدُ " O, *Zeid.*"

CHAPTER II.

OF THE ACCUSATIVE CASE.

THE following instances will exemplify the uses of the *accusative* case:

1. المَفْعُول المُطْلَق the absolute accusative, as ضَرَبْتُ ضَرْبًا "I beat *beating*;" where ضَرْبًا is the accusative of the verbal noun, and gives force to the expression.

2. المَفْعُول بِه the object of the action, as ضَرَبْتُ زَيْدًا "I beat *Zeid*."

3. المَفْعُول فِيه the time or place in which any thing is done.

Ex. سِرْتُ يَوْمًا "I travelled *one day*."

4. المَفْعُول لَه the object for which the action is performed.

Ex. ضَرَبْتُ زَيْدًا تَأْدِيبًا لَه "I have beaten Zeid for *in-struction* to him."

5. المَفْعُول مَعَه the person or thing in whose company the action was performed.

Ex. إِسْتَوَى الْمَآء وَالْخَشَبَة "The water was equal *with the wood*.

In such cases وَ *and* has the signification of مَع *with*.

The *accusative* case is also used to express the following:

1. المُنَادِي the vocative, as يَا زَيْدُ بْنَ عَمْرٍو "O, Zeid, *son* of Amr."

2. اَلْمُسْتَثْنَى the accusative of exception.

Ex. قَامَ ٱلْقَوْمِ إِلَّا زَيْدًا " The people rose *except Zeid*."

3. اَلْحَال the state or condition.

Ex. جَآءَ زَيْدٌ رَاكِبًا " Zeid came *riding*."

4. اَلتَّمْيِيز the accusative of specification.

Ex. طَابَ زَيْدٌ نَفْسًا " Zeid's *soul* was cheerful," (*lit.* Zeid was cheerful as to the soul).

5. اَلْكِنَايَة the accusative of metonymy.

Ex. كَمْ لِي عَبْدًا " *How many servants* had I ? "

عِنْدِي كَذَا دِرْهَمًا " I have *such and such dirhems*."

6. اَلْعَدَد number.

Ex. رَأَيْتُ أَحَدَ عَشَرَ رَجُلًا " I saw *eleven men*."

7. اَلتَّحْذِير caution.

Ex. اِيَّاكَ الْأَسَدَ " Take care of *the lion*."

There are several verbs signifying "to be," "to continue," &c., which require the accusative case after them, as the following :

كَانَ, as	كَانَ زَيْدٌ قَائِمًا	Zeid was standing.
اَمْسَى ..	اَمْسَى زَيْدٌ بَاكِيًا	Zeid was crying.
اَصْبَحَ ..	اَصْبَحَ زَيْدٌ ضَاحِكًا	Zeid was laughing.
اَضْحَى ..	اَضْحَى زَيْدٌ جَائِعًا	Zeid was hungry.

ظَلَّ ..	ظَلَّ زَيْدٌ تَعِبًا	Zeid was fatigued.
بات ..	بَاتَ زَيْدٌ نَادِمًا	Zeid was repenting.
لَيْسَ ..	لَيْسَ زَيْدٌ جَاهِلًا	Zeid is not ignorant.
صار ..	صَارَ زَيْدٌ عَالِمًا	Zeid was knowing.
ما زال ..	مَا زَالَ زَيْدٌ سَاهِرًا	Zeid was watching.
ما انفَكَّ ..	مَا انْفَكَّ زَيْدٌ خَاطِبًا	Zeid continued to be preaching.
ما فَتِئَ ..	مَا فَتِئَ زَيْدٌ قَارِئًا	Zeid continued reading.
ما بَرِحَ ..	مَا بَرِحَ زَيْدٌ مَاشِيًا	Zeid continued walking.
ما دام ..	تَعَلَّمْ مَا دَامَ الْعِلْمُ مُمْكِنًا	Learn as long as learning is possible.

There are several particles which have the same effect, as in the following:

انَّ ..	انَّ زَيْدًا قَائِمٌ	Zeid is standing.
كَأَنَّ ..	كَأَنَّ زَيْدًا أَسَدٌ	Zeid is as a lion.
لكِنَّ ..	قَامَ النَّاسُ لكِنَّ زَيْدًا جَالِسٌ	The people got up, but Zeid is sitting.
لَيْتَ ..	لَيْتَ زَيْدًا حَاضِرٌ	O, that Zeid were present.
لَعَلَّ ..	لَعَلَّ زَيْدًا قَادِمٌ	Perhaps Zeid is coming.

CHAPTER III.

OF THE GENITIVE CASE.

WHEN two nouns follow each other, the second being in
the genitive case, the latter is made مَجْرُور by a *casra*, as
كِتابُ الرَّجُلِ " the book of the man;" or by (ِ), as كِتابُ رَجُلٍ
" the book of a man."

The use of the genitive in Arabic is very deficient; for
if an adjective be placed after it, it may be referred either
to it, or to the preceding substantive. Thus, in the expression كتاب الرجل العظيم, the word العظيم may be taken as
a qualification either to كتاب or to الرجل. The modern
Arabs, in their vulgar conversation, seeing the defect of
this construction, remove the ambiguity by inserting the
word متاع or بتاع " property." Thus, الكتاب العظيم بتاع الرجل
" the excellent book, the property of the man;" الكتاب
بتاع الرجل العظيم " the book, the property of the excellent
man."

NOTE—The ambiguity above spoken of, arises from the
omission of the last vowels in the pronunciation, as is
usually done. Otherwise the expressions كِتَابُ ٱلرَّجُلِ ٱلْعَظِيمُ
and كِتَابُ ٱلرَّجُلِ ٱلْعَظِيمِ are sufficiently explicit.

CHAPTER IV.

OF PARTICLES WHICH AFFECT THE VERB.

In the conjugation of the verb, as given in pp. 16 and 17, the future of the indicative is exhibited only in its simplest form. It is, however, subject to the loss of the ن from these five forms, the verb taking a subjunctive signification; namely, يفعلان * تفعلان * يفعلون * تفعلون * تفعلين : the other forms will then end in a *fatha,* except the plural feminine.

The particles which make the verb subjunctive are as follows:

ان *an,* "that," as أُرِيدُ أَنْ أَكْتُبَ "I wish to write," (*lit.* "I wish that *I should write.*"

لن *lan,* "not."—Ex. لَنْ يَضْرَبَ "He will not strike." (Some say that لن is a contraction of لا ان, and the above expression is equivalent to لا يكون ان يضرب "It shall not be that he *should strike.*")

اذن *ithan,* "therefore," "then."—Ex. إِذَنْ تَدْخُلَ لِلْجَنَّـةِ "Thou mayest then enter the garden."

كي *ky* "that."—Ex. جِئْتُ كَي أَتَعَلَّمَ "I am come that I *might receive instruction.*"

حتى *'hatta,* "that," "so that."—Ex. ضَرَبْتُهُ حَتَّى يَرْجِعَ "I beat him *that he might return.*"

لِ "that," "for that."—Ex. اَتَيْتُكَ لِتَكْرَمَنِي "I came to thee, that thou mightest honour me."

او au "until."—Ex. لا افارِقُكَ او تُعطِيَنِي "I will not leave thee till thou shouldst give me," &c.

The verb is also made subjunctive when it is employed in connection with the seven following forms:

1. الاَمْر, the imperative.—Ex. زُرْنِي فَاكرِمَكَ "Visit me that I may honour thee."

2. النَهْي, the negative imperative.—Ex. لا تعصِ الشرع فتُعاقَبَ "Disobey not the law, lest thou be punished."

3. النَفْي, the negative.—Ex. لا يتكلمِ الكاذب فيكذَّبَ "Let not the liar speak, lest he be belied."

4. الاستِفْهام, the interrogation.—Ex. هَلْ ياتِي زيدٌ فيُكْرَمَ "Shall Zeid come, that he may be honoured?"

5. التَمَنِّي, desiring.—Ex. لَيتَ لِي مالًا فاَتَصَدَّقَ "O that I had wealth, that I might bestow it in alms!"

6. التَرَجِّي, hoping.—Ex. لعَلِّي اتُوب فيَغفِرَ لِي ربِّي "Perhaps I shall repent, that my Lord may forgive me."

7. اَلْعَرْض , offering.—Ex. اَلَا تَنْزِل عِنْدَنا فَتُصِيبَ خَيْرًا " Wilt thou not come down to us, *that thou mayest find good?*"

Some particles apocopate one verb, while others apocopate two verbs in connection with each other. Of the first kind we have the following, seven in number;

لَم , as	لَمْ يَكْتُبْ	He has not written.
لَمَّا ..	لَمَّا يَرْجِعْ	He has not yet returned.
اَلَمْ ..	اَلَمْ اَكْتُبْ لَكَ	Have I not written to thee?
اَلَمَّا ..	اَلَمَّا يَرْجِعْ	Has he not yet returned?
لام الامر ..	لِيَتَكَلَّمْ	Let him speak.
لا النهي ..	لا يَضْرِبْ	Let him not strike.

The following is the list of the second kind, containing ten :

ان as وِان	اِنْ تَكْتُبْ اَكْتُبْ	If thou wilt write, I will write.
ما ..	ما تَرْكَبْ اَرْكَبْ	Whatever thou ridest, I will ride.
مَن ..	مَن يُومِنْ يَخْلَص	Whosoever believeth shall be saved.
مهما ..	مَهْما تَفْعَلْ اَفْعَلْ	Whatever thou wilt do, I will do.
اَيَّ ..	اَيًّا تَضْرِبْ اَضْرِبْ	Whomsoever thou shalt beat, I will beat.

كِيفَما	كَيفَما تَتَوَجَّه تُصادِف خَيراً . .	Whithersoever thou shalt turn, thou wilt get good.
مَتي	مَتي تَرشُد تُحمَد	When thou shalt act up-rightly, thou shalt be praised.
اينما	اَينَما تَجلِس اَجلِس	In whatever place thou shalt sit, I will sit.
اَنّي	اِنّي تَفعَل اَفعَل	Wherever thou shalt act, I will act.
حيثما	حَيثُما تَتَوَجَّه اَتَوَجَّه	Wheresoever thou wilt turn, I will turn.

EXERCISES.

nák	ohanna	misat عomlil	aʿkafatt	am	bírag	nim	aw
كَان	اَنَّهُ	لِلمُعتَصِم	مَا اتَّفَق	غَرِيب	وَ مِن		
was	he that	Moعtasim the to	happened what	strange	from and		

ohagalab	af	ihiday	if	sákl	aw	ihisno	siljam	if	nadiعák
فَبَلَغَهُ	يَدِه	فِي	وَالكاس	اُنسِه	مَجلِس	فِي	قَاعِداً		
him it reached so	his hand	in	cup the and	his friends	sitting-place of	in	sitting		

ijoloع	nim	jliع	dniع	rsal	if	natafirahs	natarm	anna
عُلُوج	مِن	عِلج	عِند	الاَسر	فِي	شَرِيفَةً	اَمرَاَةً	اَنَّ
barbarians	of	a barbarian	with	bondage the	in	noble	a woman	that

E

namuoy áhihjaw alaع áhama'tal ohannaaw hayiroomaع if moorra

الـرّوم * فِي عـمُـورِيَّة وَأنَّـهُ لَـطَـمَـهـا عَـلَي وَجْـهِـهـا يَـوْمـاً

a day | her face | upon | her struck | he that | and | Amoria | in | Room the

ijay ám jliع áhal lá'k af hamiṣatعom áw ta'háṣ af

فَصـاحَت وامُـعْـتَـصِـمـاه فَقـال لَـهـا الـعِـلْـج مـا يَـجِـي

he will come | not | barbarian the | her | to | said | and | Moعtasim O | she cried so

sákl omisatعomla mata'hc'af 'kalba alaع alli ikyli

اِلَـيْـكِ اِلاَّ عَـلَي اَبْـلَـق فَـخَـتَـم الـمُـعـتَـصِـمُ الكاس

cup the | Moعtasim | sealed so | a pied horse | upon | but | you to

ikhaf dعab alli áhobarhsa ál lá'k aw i'kássil áhalawán aw

وَنـاوَلَـهـا لِـلـسّـاقِـي وَقـال لا اَشْـرُبُـهـا اِلاَّ بَـعْـد فَـكّ

delivery after | but | it | I will drink | not | said and | cup-bearer | to the | it gave and

'hab'sa ammal af jliع ilta'kaw rsala nim hafírahshs

الـشّـرِيـفَـة مِـن الأسْـر وَقَـتْـل الـعِـلْـج فَـلَـمّـا اَصْـبَـح

he was in the morning | when and | barbarian the | kill-ing | and bondage | the | from | noble the | of

jorhćay ál na oharaksaع rama aw —— ali lí'harrib adán

نـادَي بِـالـرّحِـيـل اِلَي عموريّة وَأمَـر عَـسْـكَـرهُ اَن لا يَـخْـرُج

go out | not that | his troops | ordered and | Amoria | to | marching the | for called

fla niعbas if oojaraháć af 'kalba alaع alli mohnim da'ha

اَحَـد مِـنْـهُـم اِلاَّ عَـلَي اَبْـلَـق فَـخَـرَجُـوا فِي سَـبْـعِـيـن اَلْـف

1000 | 70 | in | they went out so | a pied horse | upon | but | them of | one

---

* All the European nations, with the inhabitants of Asia Minor, are often called Romans by the Arabian writers.

—— 'htafíb hylaع aláعat hállA 'hataf ammal af 'kalba

اَبۡلَق فَلَـمّـا فَـتَحَ اَللّٰهُ تَعَالَى عَلَـيۡهِ بِـفَـتۡحِ عموربة

Amoria opening by him upon be high God opened when and ——

jliعla bala'taw —— ikybbal loo'kay awhaw áhalahćad

دَخَـلَـهَا وَهۡوَ يَـقُولُ لَبَّيۡكِ لَبَّيۡكِ وَطَـلَب العلج

—— sought and —— here I am says he and her he entered (it)

—— dooyo'k kkaf aw oha'knoع abara'd af hafírahshs arisá

آسِــرَ الشَّـرِيۡفة فَـضَـرَبَ عُنۡقَهُ وَفَـكَّ قُيُودَ الشريفة

—— bonds loosed and his neck struck and noble the of imprisoner

dhib oháta af isák nála il itáh i'kássil lá'k aw

وَقَال لِلسَّـاقِي هاتِ لِي اَلآنَ كاسِي فَـاَتَاهُ بِـهَا

her with came he so my cup now me to bring cup-bearer to the said and (it) him to

obárahshs abá't nála lá'k aw birahs aw áhamtahć kkaf af

فَـفَكَّ خَتۡمَـهَا وَشَـرِب وَقال الانَ طَـابَ الشَّـرَابُ *

drink the it is good now said and drank and her seal broke and (its)

ANECDOTE OF MOعTASÍM.

AND this was one of the strange adventures which happened to Moعtasím: that he was sitting in an assembly of his friends, with a cup in his hand; and it was reported to him that a noble lady was in bondage with a barbarian of the barbarians of Rome, in Ammoria, and that he had struck her on the face one day, and she cried, "Help, O Moعtasim!" And the barbarian said to her, "He will not come to you unless on a pied horse." And Mo‿taśim sealed up the cup, and gave it to the cup-bearer, and said, " By heaven, I will not drink of it till after the delivery of the lady from bondage, and the death of the barbarian." And when it was morning, he gave orders for marching against Ammoria, and commanded his troops that not one man of them should go forth except on a pied horse: and they set out upon seventy thousand pied horses. And when he conquered, by the taking of Ammoria, he entered it, and he said, " Here I am, here I am;" and he sought the barbarian, the imprisoner of the lady, and struck off his head; and he loosed the bonds of the lady, and said to the cup-bearer, " Bring me now my cup;" and he approached him with it, and he broke the seal of it, and drank, and said, " Now delicious is the wine."

الليلة الثانية والستون بعد المائة من حكايات الف ليلة وليلة

áhithćo il dáz ánid talák´ halibá´kla halylla tanák ammalaf

فَلَـمَّا كانَت اللَّيْـلَة القابِـلة قـالَت دينا زاد لِأُخْـتِـهـا

her sister to zad Dina said following the night the was when and

ánal immita af hamián aryg itnok ni hátćho áy dázrhahs

شَـهـرزاد يا أُخْـتـاه ان كُـنْـتِ غَيْـرَ نائِمَةٍ فَاَتِـمِّي لَـنـا

us for finish asleep not you were if sister O Zad Shahr *kilaml áhoia inagalab hamárak aw nabbo'h áhal talá'k htida'hla*

الْحَدِيْث قَالَت لَهَا حُبًّا وَكَرَامَه بَلَغَنِي اَيَّها الْمَلِك

king the O me reached It honour and love her to she said story the

ohanni af simáhćl icha ámma aw lá'k niyyazoml anna di assa

السَّعِيْد اَنَّ الْمُزَيِّنَ قال وَاَمَّا اَخِــي الْخَامِس فَاِنَّــهُ

he that 5th the my brother as to and said barber the that happy the

sánn olasay narí'kaf nalojar nák wa ináthál a oot'kam nák

كان مَقْطُوع الآذانِ وكان رَجُلٌ فَقِيْرًا يَسْأَل النَّاس

men the begs of poor man was and ears the cut was

ánodiláw nák aw naráhan ohohtohćay ámib otát'kay aw nalyl

لَيْلًا وَيَقْتَات بِمَا يَاخُذُهُ نَهَارًا وكانَ والدُّنا

our father was and day it takes he that by subsists and night

fallahć aw tám aw llat af nniss if nani át' naribak nahćyhs

شَيْخًا كَبِيْرًا طَاعِنًا فِي السِّنِّ فَاعْتَلَّ وَمات وخَلَّف

left and died and fell ill so the age in going far great old

llok htahća af ánanyb áhánmasat'k af mahrid haima bas ánal

لَنا سَبْعُمِائَة دِرْهَم فَاقْتَسَمْناها بَيْنَنا فَاخَذ كُل

every took and us between her we divided and dirhems 700 us to
(it)

ahtahća ohanni af simáhćla ihća amma af mahrid ha'im di'háw

واحِد مِائَة دِرْهَم فَاَمّا اَخِــي الْخَامِس فَاِنَّهُ اَخَذ

took he that 5th the my brother as to and dirhems 100 one

ámanyb aw áhib la ćfay ám irday mal aw rát'h aw miháradd

الــدَّراهِم وَاْحْتار وَلَم يَدْرِ ما يَفْعَل بِها وَبَيْنَما

whilst and her by does he what knows not and amazed is and money the
it   (it)

na ihiri'táhc if ɛa'kaw hti miháradd aklit if rakkafatay awoh

هُوَ يَتَفَكَّرُ فِي تِلْكَ الدَّرَاهِمِ اذ وَقَعَ فِي خَاطِرِهِ اَنْ

that his mind in fell when money the that in thinks he

ɛifatnay aw ohaɛibay aw ɛuon llok nim najájoz áhib irathsay

يَشْتَرِي بِهَا زُجَاجًا مِنْ كُلِّ نَوْعٍ وَيَبِيعَهُ وَيَنْتَفِع

gain and it sell and sort every of glass her with he will buy
(it)

daɛak'aw ríbak 'kaba't if ohalaɛaj aw jájozz araths af ihib

بِهِ فَاشْتَرَى الزُّجَاجَ وَجَعَلَهُ فِي طَبَقٍ كَبِيرٍ وَقَعَدَ

sat and large basket in it put and glass the he purchased so it by

oharhaht dansa af 'ti á'h ihibináj ali aw hnim ɛíbay i'duom if

فِي مَوْضِعٍ يَبِيعُ مِنْهُ وَالَى جَانِبِهِ حَائِطٌ فَأَسْنَدَ ظَهْرَهُ

his back leant and wall his side to and it of sell place in

sfan áy imalɛi ihisfan if lák af rikatfay adaɛa'k aw ihyla

عَلَيْهِ وَقَعَدَ يَفْتَكِرُ فَقَالَ فِي نَفْسِهِ اَعْلَمِي يَانَفْس

soul O know him self in said and thinks sat and it upon

mahrid haimɛabra ib ohoɛiba jájozz átháh ilám asar nna

اَنَّ رَأْسَ مَالِي هَذَا الزُّجَاجَ اَبِيعُهُ بِاَرْبَعِمَائَةِ دِرْهَم

dirhems 400 for it I sell glass this my money (of) head that

idniɛ lassa'hatay na ali ɛiba aw írathsa oláza al inni ammoht

ثُمَّ اِنِّي لَا اَزَالُ اَشْتَرِي وَاَبِيعُ اِلَى اَنْ يَتَحَصَّلَ عِنْدِي

me with there reach that till sell and buy I cease not I that then

ali aholim'ha aw ɛiá'dab ahib iratsha af mahrid fálá taɛabra

اَرْبَعَةُ آلَافِ دِرْهَم فَاشْتَرِي بِهَا بَضَائِعَ وَاَحْمِلُهَا اِلَى

to her carry and goods her by buy (it) and ———— 1000 4
(them) (it)

*âl ammoht mahrid fâlâ tayinámaht ib áho*ع*iba aw áthak* ع*ّduom*

مَوْضِع كَذا وَاَبِيْعِها بِثَمانِيَة آلاف دِرْهَم ثُمَّ لا

not then —— 1000 8 for her sell and such place
(them)

ع*imaj nim ahif arc̓ho ha*ع*á'dib iratsha atta'h oláza*

اَزالُ حَتَّي اَشْتَرِي بِضاعَة اُخْرَي فِيْها مِن جَمِيْع

all of her in other merchandise I buy until desist

*na'hbir áhib 'habra aw áho*ع*iba af r̓ti*ع*la fánsa aw rihâwajla*

الْجَواهِر وَاَصْناف الْعِطْر فَاَبِيْعُها وَاَرْبَح بِها رِبْحًا

gain her by gain and her sell and perfumes (of) kinds and jewels
(them) (them)

*kilámam aw hanasa'h narâd írathsa kiláht dni*ع *af nalízaj*

جَزِيْلًا فَعِنْد ذَلِك اَشْتَرِي دارًا حَسَنَة وَمَمالِيْك

attendants and fine a house I will buy that at and much

illahc̓o ál aw fis̓ka aw barhsa aw loká aw nalyhc̓ aw namadahc̓ aw

وَخَدَمًا وَخَيْلًا وَآكُل وَاَشْرَب وَاَقْصف وَ لا اُخَلِّي

leave not and make and drink and eat and horses and servants and
merry

mohotra'd'haaw alli hanídaml if hayinnagom âl aw nainnagom

مُغَنِّيًا وَلا مُغَنِّيَة فِي الْمَدِينَة اِلَّا وَاَحْضَرْتُهم

them I brought but city in female-singer —— male-singer

*haim alâ*ع*at hállA áhs ni ílám sár la*ع*ja aw idni*ع

عِنْدِي وَاَجْعَل راس مالِي اِن شا اللّٰه تَعالَي مائَة

100 be high God wish if my money head make and me to

o'kaba'taw ihiláb if hobos̓hay —— ohollok áthâh mahrid fla

الف دِرْهَم هَذا كُلَّه كان يَحْسُبُه فِي بالِه وَطَبَق

basket and his mind in it reckons was he all this —— 1000
(of) he

abasa'h ohanni ammoht mahrid　　haimlib　　hyday　　nyb　　jájozz

الزّجاج بـين يَدَيـه بالمائة دِرهَم ثُمَّ انّـهُ حَسَبَ

reckoned that　then　——　100　by his hands　between　glass

dni'af mahrid fla haim ilám rás áhti aw lá'k áw

وقـال واذا صـار مـالي مائَة ألَف دِرهَم فَعند

at　——　1000　100　my money　became　when and　said and

tánab bo't́cha aw ba'tohćl if tálálladd otha'ba kiláht

ذَلك اَبَعثُ الـدَّلَّالات في الخُـطَب وأَخْـطُب بَنات

daughters demand in and weddings　in female brokers　I send　that
　　　　　　　　marriage

na'ع inagalab da'kaf ánorîzaw ámayisál aw árazowl áw koolomla

المُلُوك والـوُزَرآ ولاسِـيَّـما وِزِـيـرُنا فَـقَد بَـلَـغَـني عَن

of　it me reached　as　our vizir　especially　vizirs　and kings

ta'hílam nso'hl otaعídab fáśuol otalimák áhanna ihitnib

بِنتـهُ انّـها كامِلةُ الأوَصاف بَـدِيـعةُ الحُـسْن مَلِيحة

beautiful　beauty (of) wonderful　descriptions (of) perfect she　that　his daughter

álli aw nák oo'dar ni af ránid fla áhorihmo áw fár'ta la

الأطْـراف وأمْـهَـرُها ألَف دِيـنار فـان رَضُـوا كان والّا

not if and was　they consent　if and　dinars　1000　her offer and　　ends

irád if talaśa'h áhti af áhíba fna mgar alaع áhothtahća

اَخَـذْتُـها عَلَي رَغْـم ألَف أبِيـها فـاذا حَصَلَت في داري

my house in　she got　if and　her father　nose　putting in　upon　her I took
　　　　　　　　　the dust

koololm atawsok irathsa ammoht rágí's máddohć harahsaع irathsa

اَشْـتَري عَشَرَة خُدّام صِغار ثُمَّ اَشْتَري كُسوةَ المُلُوك

king's　robes　——　then　young　servants　10　I will buy

ammoht nimhtomla rahoujli b   naɛassarom   bahath   nim   najras aw

وَسَرْجًا مِن ذَهَب مُرَصَّعًا بِالجَوْهَرِ المُثْمِن ثُمَّ

then | of value | jewels by | set | gold | of | saddle and

inámay naɛaw imáddo'k aw íflahć kilámaml obikkaro

أَرْكَبُ المَمالِيك خَلْفِي وقُدَّامِي وعَن يَمِيني

my right | on and | me before and | me behind | attendants | I make ride

ohanákam inadaɛ'ka aw il má'k inâar áthi af ilámihs aw

وشَمالِي فَاذا رآنِي قام لِي وأَقْعَدَني مَكانَهُ

his place | and caused me to sit | me for | stood | me he saw | when and | my left and

iɛam htohćá aw horhiś inna il inood awoh daɛak'aw

وقَعَد هُوَ دُونِي لأَنِّي صِهْرُهُ وآخُذ مَعِي

me with | I take and | his son-in-law | I because | me below | he | sat and

rhamlil ránid áfla amihíf nysík ámoholimmáho aw nymidáhć

خادِمَين وأَحْمِلُهما كِيسَين فِيهِما أَلْفا دِينار لِلْمَهْر

portion for | ———— | 2000 | them in | two purses | them load and | two servants

ísfan rbik oomalɛay atta'h rahćá ránid fla idho aw

وأُهْدِي أَلْف دِينار آخَر حَتَّي يَعْلَمُوا كِبَر نَفْسِي

my soul (of) | greatness | they know | so that | other | 1000 | I give and

irád ali firaśna ammoht inyɛ if áynodd aragis aw

وصِغَر الدُّنْيا فِي عَيْني ثُمَّ انْصَرِف إِلَي دارِي

my house | to | I retire | then | my eye | in | world (of) | smallness and

tɛalahć aw ohal tbahaw itarm itayi'hán nim da'ha áj ahti af

فَاذا جاآ أَحَد مِن ناحِيَة امْرَاتِي وهَبْت لَهُ وخَلَعْت

clothed and | him to | I gave | my woman (of) | side | from | one | came when and

*inni ammoht hyla*ع *ahotdadar hayidahib áj ni aw ihyla*ع

عَلَیْهِ وَاِنْ جَا بِهَدِیَّة رَدَدْتُهَا عَلَیْهِ ثُمَّ اِنِّي

I   then   him upon   it I gave back   a present by   came   if and   him upon

*mohotrama kiláht oola*ع*af áhti af ináhs 'hálśi ib mohoromá*

آمُرُهُــم بِاِصْلاح شَانِي فَاِذَا فَعَلُوا ذَلِك أَمَرْتُهم

I commanded them that they did when and state my to arrange them command

hawlahél ot'kaw áj áhti af írád hálśi aw áhifáfiz ib

بِزِفَافِهَا وَاِصْلاح دَارِي فَاِذَا جَا وَقْت الخَلْوة

retirement (of) time came when and my house to arrange and to go in procession with her

*jábíd habatram ala*ع *ta*ع*a'k aw íbáyiht rahéfa tsibal itarmib*

بِأَمْرَاقِي لَبِسْت أَفْخَر ثِیَابِي وَقَعَدت عَلَي مَرْتَبة دِیبَاج

silk cushion upon sat — —clothes the best I put on with my wife

ímli'h roofo il nalámihs ál aw nanímay tifatla ál naikattom

مُتَّكِئًا لا اَلْتَفت یَمِینًا وَلا شِمَالاً لِوُفُور حِلْمِي

prudence much for left nor right turn — — reclining

áhilalohaw áhayilóh if rdabl ak hamiá'k ítarm onookat aw ítanázar aw

وَرِزَانَتِي وتَكُون أَمْرَاقِي قَائِمة كَالْبَدْر فِي حُلِیَّهَا وَحُلَلَهَا

robes ornaments in moon like standing — wife she will be gravity —

nam ع*ímaj loo'kay atta'h nafalá's aw narbik áhyli rohtna ál ána aw*

وَاَنَا لا اَنْظُر اِلَیْهَا كِبْرًا وَصَلَفًا حَتَّي یَقُول جَمِیع مَن

who all say so that pride for pride her to look — — I

*áhyla*ع *fa'tta*ع*at katayiráj aw katarmi ánáluom aw ánadiys áy ra'da'h*

حَــضَــر یَاسَیِّدْنَا وَمَوْلانَا اِمْرَاتك وَجَارِیتك تَعَطّف عَلَیْهَا

her upon bend pity thy maid — thy wife — lord — our master was present

harhtan iɓ áhyla‛ mi‛na kyday nyb hamiá‛k áhanni af

فَاِنَّهَا قَائِمَة بَيْن يَدَيْكِ اَنْعِم عَلَيْهَا بِنَظْرَة

a look — upon favour thy 2 hands between standing she for

áhyli rohtna aw isár ‛afra kiláht dni‛ af máyi‛kl áhib rra'da da‛k af

فَقَد اَضَرِّ بِهَا القِيام فَعِنْد ذَلِك اَرْفِع راسي وَاَنْظُر اِلَيْها

— look — — head I raise that at standing hurt for

riygoaw ána moo'ka af áhitarjo'h ali áhib noo'dmay af hadi'háw harhtan

نَظْرَه واحِدَة فَيَمْضُون بِها اِلَي حُجَرَتها فَاَقُوم اَنا وَاُغَيِّر

change and I I rise up her room to — they go and one — look

hayináhthta harraml itaáj ahti af áhnim nas'ha sabla ammoht íhsámo'k

قُماشي ثُمّ اَلْبَس اَحْسَن مِنْها فَاذا جآت النَمَرّة الثّانية

second time came — she than better put on then — clothes (they)

ayyday nyb oofi'kay atta'h áhylli rohtna al hayináhthta ha‛lihé lib

بِالْخِلْعَة الثّانِيَة لا اَنْظُر اِلَيْها حَتّي يَقِفُوا بَيْن يَدَّيْ

my 2 hands between they stand till to I look not — — robe

ammoht iny‛ fara'tib áhyli rohtna af rárim haddi‛ inoolasay w

وَيَسْأَلُوني عِدَّة مِرار فَاَنْظُر اِلَيْها بِطَرَف عَيْني ثُمّ

then my eye corner I look times several me ask

áhotawlaj mmitat atta'h kiláhtak láza ál aw 'dral ali 'kir'to

اُطْرِق اِلَي الاَرْض ولا اَزال كَذَلِك حَتّي تَتِمّ جَلوتها

decoration finish till likewise desist earth bend my eyes

haimosmahé hif nasik oomidda'koy na máddohéla'd‛ab romá ínni ammoht

ثُمّ اني آمُر بَعْض الْخُدّام اَن يُقَدّمُوا كِيسًا فيه خَمْسُمائة

500 it in purse they bring that servants some command then

áhib inoolhćoy na mohoromā ammoht 'tihsáwaml ali ohoɛafda af ránid

دِينار فَادْفَعُهُ إِلَى المَوَاشِطِ ثُمَّ آمُرُهُمْ أَن يُخَلُّونِي بِها

—— let me alone —— —— —— tire women to it gave and

ál aw áhibináj ali māna aw áhyli rohtna áhib oolahćad áthi af

فَاذا دَخَلُوا بِها اَنْظُرُ اِلَيْها وَاَنامُ اِلِي جانِبِها وَلا

—— her side to sleep and her to I look —— they went in ——

íjat af haríbak isfan nni ínnaɛ láḱoy atta'h áhomillako

أُكَلِّمُها حَتَّى يُقالَ عَنِّي اِن نَفْسِي كَبِيْرَة فَنَجِي

will come and great —— Soul that of me it may be said that her to spea

ali rohtno ídiys ây loo´kat aw íday libba´kot af áhommo

أُمَّها فَتُقَبِّل يَدِي وَتَقُول ياسَيِّدِي اُنْظُر اِلِي

to look my master O say and my hand kiss and her mother

ál af áharítáhć robja w kabro´k íhathsat áhanni af kitayirâj

جارِيَتِكَ فانَها تَشْتَهِي قُرْبَكَ وَاَجْبُر خاطِرَها فَلا

—— mind recover approaching wishes she for thy maid

soobat af moo´kat ínnim kiláth taar áhti af nabâwaj áhylaɛddora

أُرُدّ عَلَيْها جَوابًا فَاذا رَاَت ذَلِك مِنِّي تَقُوم فَتَبُوس

she will she rises me from that saw if answer —— give
kiss back

tâar ám aw hayibás ítanbi ídiys ây loo´kat aw narárim íljir

رِجْلِي مِرارًا وَتَقُول ياسَيِّدِي اِبْنَتِي صَبِيَّة وَما رَاَت

saw not young my daughter my master O say several my foot
times

áhobla´k risaknay 'dábi´knila kiláht knim tâar áhti af nalojar

رَجُلًا فَاذا رَاَت مِنْك ذَلِك الاِنْقِباض يَنْكَسِر قَلْبُها

her heart break frown that thee from she saw if and man

áhi′tᵉot — áharitâhćaw áhabla′k biy′t aw áhmillak aw áhyli lim af

فَمِلْ اِلَيْها وَكَلِّمْها وَطَيِّب قَلْبَها وخاطِرها ثُمَّ تُعْطِيها

her she give then mind heart sooth speak her to bend so

kidiysᵉ alaᵍ ífil′hi áhal loo′kat aw bârahs ihif na′hadá′k áhommo

أُمُّها قَدَحاً فِيْهِ شَراب وَتَقُول لَها اُحْلِفِي عَلَيّ سَيِّدِكٍ

thy lord upon conjure her to say wine it in cup her mother

ayyday nyb hamiá′k áhokorta ínta áj áhti af hi′ks aw

واسْقِيْه فاذا جاۤئَنِي اَتْرُكُها قائِمَة بَيْنَ يَدَيَّ

my 2 hands between standing her I leave me came if give him to drink

ínni loo′kat atta′h ísfan rbik nim áhyli rohtna ál ikattom âna aw

وَاَنا مُتَّكِي لا اَنْظُرِ اِلَيْها مِن كِبْرِ نَفْسِي حَتَّي تَقُول اَنِي

she says until Soul pride —— look — reclining I and

ayyday nyb hamiá′k áhillahćo aw hazíza ᵍ ísfan aw zíza ᵍ

عَزيز وَنَفْسِي عَزِيْزَة وَاُخَلِّيها قائِمَة بَيْنَ يَدَيَّ

my 2 hands between standing her leave I —— powerful

íl loo′kat af nâ′tlos ínna mal ᵍat aw nâwahla m ᵍa′t ‛koohtat il

لِتَـذُوق طَعْم الهَوان وَتَعْلَم اَنِّي سُلْطان فَتَقُول لِي

she says sultan know subjection (of) taste she may taste that

íday nim ‛hada′kl iddorat ál kyla ᵍ háll i′k′ka′hib ídiys áy

ياسَيِّدِي بِحَقّ اللَّه عَلَيْكَ لا تَـرُدّ القَدَح مِن يَدِي

—— cup give back thee upon God (of) truth by my lord O

addob ál loo′kat aw ayyla ᵍ ‛hilot af áhomillako álaf katayirâj âna aw

وَاَنا جارِيَتَكَ فَلا اُكَلِّمْها فَتُلِحّ عَلَيَّ وَتَقُول لابُـدَّ

escape — —— me upon she urges I speak — thy slave —

áhihjaw íf íday ´dofna af ímaf ali hobirra´kot aw ihibrohs nim

مِن شُرْبِهِ وتُقَرِّبِـهِ اِلِي فَمِي فَاَنْفُض يَدِي فِي وَجْهِها

her face | in | I shake | my mouth | she brings it near | drink

tââj af ihiljirib safar ammoht âhtakâh lamҀa aw íljirib áhosofra aw

وَاَرْفُسُها بِرِجْلِي واَعْمَل هَكَذا ثُـمَّ رَفَس بِرِجْلِه فَجات

came and | spurned | then | so | make | my foot | with her spurn

´dral inaҀ Ҁifatrom nâkam íf nák aw jâjozz í´kaba´t alaҀ

عَلَي طَبَـقِ الـزّجاج وكان فِي مَكان مُرتَفِع عَنِ الأَرْض

earth | of | high | place | it was | glass | (of) basket upon

ihíf âm llok rassakat aw ´dral ali lazan af

فَـنَـزَل اِلَي الأَرْض وتَكَسَّر كُلَّما فِيهِ *

it in | that all | broke | ground | to | it went down

THE HUNDRED AND SIXTY-SECOND NIGHT OF THE TALES

OF A THOUSAND AND ONE NIGHTS.

WHEN the following night arrived, Dinazad said to Shahrzad, " O, sister! if you are not asleep, finish to us the story." She replied to her with great pleasure, " It is related to me, O king of exalted dignity, that the barber spoke thus: ' As to my fifth brother, he was crop-eared, and was a poor man, who begged in the evening, and subsisted on that by day. Our father was an old man, greatly advanced in years, when he fell sick and died, leaving to us 700 dirhems, which we divided, each 100 dirhems. As to my fifth brother, when he received the dirhems he was amazed, and did not know what he should do with them. But whilst he was meditating upon the money, it came into his mind to buy with it glass of every kind, and to retail and gain by it. He purchased, therefore, glass, and put it into a large basket, and seated himself in a place in which he might sell it. And by his side was a wall; and he leant his back against it, and sat meditating and saying to himself, Know, O soul, that the capital amount of this glass I sell for 400 dirhems. Then, however, I will not stop: I will buy and sell till there remain with me 4000 dirhems; and I will carry it to such and such a place, and will sell it for 8000 dirhems. Then I will not give over till I buy goods as before; and I will purchase with it in wholesale jewels and perfumes, and I will acquire great gain. Then after that I will purchase a fine house, and I will buy slaves, and attendants, and horses; and I will eat, and I will drink, and I will make merry; and I shall neither want for the male singer nor the female singers of the city, but make them to come to me; and I will increase, God willing, my capital sum to 100,000 dirhems. All this he reckoned in his imagination, with the basket of glass before him of 100 dirhems. Then he still computed in his mind, and said, When it shall become a capital of 100,000 dirhems, then upon that I will send out female brokers in marriage, and I will demand in marriage daughters of kings and vizirs;

particularly of our vizir, as it is reported to me concerning her that she is perfect in accomplishments, wonderful in beauty, and graceful in shape; and I will offer to her a portion of 1000 dinars. If they consent, let it be; but if not, I will carry her away, in defiance of her father's anger, by force; then, when I have got her into my house, I will purchase for her ten young slaves: afterwards I will buy robes of princes, and a saddle of gold, adorned with jewels of value. Then I will cause the servants to ride behind me and before me; and I will go round the city, and the people will salute me and will pray for me. And then I will return and enter to the vizir, servants behind me and before me, and on my right hand and on my left; and when he sees me he will stand before me, and will cause me to sit in his seat, and place himself below me, because I am his son-in-law. And I will take with me two slaves, and I will load them with two purses, in which will be 2000 dinars, which I shall cause to be counted out as her portion; and I will present 1000 dinars afterwards, that they may know my generosity and my greatness of soul, and the littleness of the world in my eyes. Then I will return to my house; and if one shall come on the part of my wife, I will present to him and clothe him with a rich dress; and if he comes with a gift, I will throw it to him, and will not receive it from him, and I will not leave myself but in a respectful place.

And when these things are performed, I will go to them, and give them orders for the marriage night, and for the arrangement of my house. Then when the hour comes for retirement with my bride, I will dress in my most magnificent robes; and I will sit in dignity, reclining upon a silk cushion, not turning to the right or to the left, with grave prudence and majestic wisdom, and solemnity in my words; and there will be my spouse standing like the full moon in her robes and ornaments, and I will not look upon her, out of pride and respect, so that all those who are present will say, Oh our lord and our master, bend towards your spouse and your servant, for she is standing before you : favour her with a look : standing is indeed painful to her. Then they will kiss the ground before me many times, on which I will raise my head and look upon her with a single glance : then I will turn away and recline my head. They will then retire with her to her chamber, and I will also rise up, and I will change my clothes. Then I will dress more handsomely ; and when she comes a second time in second robes I will not look on her till they stand before me, and entreat me as before. Then I will look upon her with the corner of my eye ; after which I will bend my eyes upon the ground, and I will not desist thus till her decoration is completed. Then I will order some of the servants to bring a purse with 500 dinars, and I will give it to the tire-women : then I will order

them to leave me alone with her. When they have
brought her in, then I will look at her, and I will sleep
by her side, and not speak to her. So that mention will
be made of me, as to the haughtiness of my mind, and
her mother will come and will kiss my hand, and say,
Oh, my lord, look upon your servant, as she wishes to
approach you and recover her spirits: but I will not give
her any answer. And when she perceives that from me,
she will remain kissing my feet, and will say, ' Oh, my
lord, my daughter is a virgin, and never saw man: when,
therefore, she perceives from you those frowns, it will
break her heart. Bend to her, then, and speak to her, and
soothe her heart and her mind. Then her mother will
give her a cup of wine, and will say to her, Take this cup
to your lord, and present it to him. When she ap-
proaches me I will let her stand before me, whilst I,
reclining, will not look at her, from the pride of my heart;
so that she will say that I am proud, and my soul is
proud; whilst I will not relax, but leave her standing
before me, that she may taste distress, and know that I
am sultan, and say to me, Oh, my lord, by the truth of
God do not refuse the cup from my hand, I am your
servant; and I will not speak to her. Then she will beg
me earnestly, and she will say, You must drink it; and
she will advance it to my mouth, and I will shake my
hand in her face, and spurn her with my foot. My
brother, being thus employed, pushed with his foot, and

struck with violence upon the basket of glass, which, being on a place elevated above the ground, fell upon the pavement, and broke all that was in it.' "

اسمآ الشهور		THE MONTHS OF THE YEAR.
(ك) كانون الثاني	*cânoon aththâni,*	January.
شباط	*shobâ't,*	February.
ادار	*âdâr,*	March.
نيسان	*nisân,*	April.
ايار	*iyâr,*	May.
حزيران	*hazîrân,*	June.
تموز	*tammouz,*	July.
اب	*âb,*	August.
ايلول	*ilool,*	September.
(ت) تشرين الاول	*tishreen al-ouwal,*	October.
(ت) تشرين الثاني	*tishreen aththâni,*	November.
(ك) كانون الاول	*Cânoon al-ouwal,*	December.

ايام الاسبوع		THE DAYS OF THE WEEK.
الاحد	*al-a'had,*	Sunday.
الاثنين	*al-ithnine,*	Monday.
الثلاثا	*aththalâtha,*	Tuesday.
الاربعا	*al-arbaعa,*	Wednesday.
الخميس	*al-ćhamîs,*	Thursday.
الجمعه	*al-jomعah,*	Friday.
السبت	*assabt,*	Saturday.

اسماَ العدد   CARDINAL NUMBERS.

واحد	*wáʼhid,*	one.
اثنين	*ithnine,*	two.
ثلثة	*thaláthah,*	three.
اربعه	*arbaɛah,*	four.
خمسه	*ćhamsah,*	five.
سته	*sittah,*	six.
سبعه	*sabɛah,*	seven.
ثمانيه	*thamániyah,*	eight.
تسعه	*tisɛah,*	nine.
عشرة	*ɛasharah,*	ten.
احد عشر	*iʼhda ɛshar,*	eleven.
اثنا عشر	*ithna ɛshar,*	twelve.
ثلثة عشر	*thalata ɛshar,*	thirteen.
اربعة عشر	*arbaɛta ɛshar,*	fourteen.
خمسة عشر	*ćhamsata ɛshar,*	fifteen.
ستة عشر	*sittata ɛshar,*	sixteen.
سبعة عشر	*sabɛata ɛshar,*	seventeen.
ثمانية عشر	*thamanita ɛshar,*	eighteen.
تسعة عشر	*tisɛata ɛshar,*	nineteen.
عشرين	*ɛishreen,*	twenty.
ثلثين	*thalátheen,*	thirty.
اربعين	*arbaɛeen,*	forty.
خمسين	*ćhamseen,*	fifty.
ستين	*sitteen,*	sixty.
سبعين	*sabɛeen,*	seventy.

اسمآ العدد		CARDINAL NUMBERS.
ثمانين	thamâneen,	eighty.
تسعين	tiṣeen,	ninety.
مائة	miyah,	a hundred.
الف	alf,	one thousand.

العدد النعت		ORDINAL NUMBERS.
اول	awal,	first.
ثاني	thâni,	second.
ثالث	thâlith,	third.
رابع	râbiʿ,	fourth.
خامس	châmis,	fifth.
سادس	sâdis,	sixth.
سابع	sâbiʿ,	seventh.
ثامن	thâmin,	eighth.
تاسع	tâsiʿ,	ninth.
عاشر	ʿâshir,	tenth.
حادي عشر	hâdi ʿashr,	eleventh.
ثاني عشر	thâni ʿashr,	twelfth.
ثالث عشر	thâlith ʿashr,	thirteenth.
رابع عشر	râbiʿ ʿashr,	fourteenth.
خامس عشر	châmis ʿashr,	fifteenth.
سادس عشر	sâdis ʿashr,	sixteenth.
سابع عشر	sâbiʿ ʿashr,	seventeenth.
ثامن عشر	thâmin ʿashr,	eighteenth.
تاسع عش	tâsiʿ ʿashr,	nineteenth.
عشرون	ʿishroon,	twentieth.

العدد الجمعي

زوج	zouje,	a couple.
نصف دوزينه	niʹsf doozinah,	half-a-dozen.
عشرين	ɛishreen,	a score.
مائة	miyah,	a hundred.
الف	alf,	a thousand.
النصف	anniśf,	the half.
الثلث	aththolth,	the third.
الربع	arrobɛ,	{ a quarter, or a fourth.
لخمس	al-ćhoms,	a fifth.
ثلثين	tholthine,	two thirds.
ثلثة ارباع	thalâthat arbâɛ,	three fouths.
اربعة اخماس	arbaɛat aéhmâs,	four fifths.
مضاعف * مزوج	moḋâɛaf, mozwij,	double.
مثلث	mothallath,	treble.
مربّع	morabbaɛ,	fourfold.

القياس والكيل

قنطار	ʹkinʹtâr,	quintal.
رطل	raʹtl,	pound.
اوقية	ouʹkiyah,	ounce.
درهم	dirham,	dram.
ذراع	thirâɛ,	yard.
قيراط * اصبع	iśbaɛ, ʹkirâʹt,	inch.
قدم	ʹkadam,	foot.

باع	*bâ*ع,	fathom.
ميل	*meel,*	mile.
فدان	*faddân,*	acre.

1	2	3	4	5	6	7	8	9	10
١	٢	٣	٤	٥	٦	٧	٨	٩	١٠

DIALOGUES.

FIRST DIALOGUE.

ARABIC PARLANCE.	PRONUNCIATION.	ENGL. EQUIVALENTS.
صباح الخير ياسيدي	*'sabâ'h al-ćhire yâ sidi,*	Good morning, Sir.
ايش حالك	*aish 'hâlak,*	How are you?
طيب بخير الله يسلمك	*'ty-ib bi'chire Allah yosallimak,*	Well—may God save you.
كيف اصبحتم	*keif aṣba'htom,*	How were you in the morning?
الحمد لله داعي لكم	*al'hamdu lillâh dâ*ع*i lakom,*	Praise be to God, praying for you.
هل عندك اخبار	*hal*ع*indak aćhbâr,*	Have you any news?

ARABIC PARLANCE.	PRONUNCIATION.	ENGL. EQUIVALENTS.
لا شي مهم	lâ shy mohimm,	Nothing of importance.
هل سمعت شي	hal samiɛt shy,	Have you heard any thing?
كيف (ايش) حال اخوك	keif (aish) 'hâl achook,	How is your brother?
مريض جدًّا	marîd jiddan,	Very ill.
شفاه الله	shafâh Allah,	May God cure him!
اين (فاين) كنت الايام دي	aine (fa-aine) cont al eyyâm di,	Where were you these days?
كنت مشغول	cont mashgool,	I was busy.
هل شفت فلان	hal shoft folân,	Did you see So-and-so?
نعم شفته	naɛam shoftoh,	Yes, I saw him.
ايش يعمل هناك	aish yaɛmal honâc,	What is he doing there?
يتعلم	yetɛallam,	He is studying.
متي يجي هنا	mata yajî honâ,	When will he come here?
غدا	gada,	To-morrow.
سلم عليه من عندي	sallim ɛalieh min ɛindi,	Salute him on my part.

ARABIC PARLANCE.	PRONUNCIATION.	ENGL. EQUIVALENTS.
وقل له اني مشتاق اليه	wa'kol loh inni moshtâk ilieh,	And tell him that I am desiring to see him.
ما انسيش	ma ansash,	I will not forget.
مع السلامه	maعassalâmah,	Go in peace.

SECOND DIALOGUE.

يا ولد طلع الفجر	yâ walad 'talâعal fajr,	Boy, is it morning?
الشمس طلعت من زمان	ashshams 'talaعat min zamân,	The sun has risen for some time.
لما افتح الطاقه تشوف	lammâ afta'h at-tâعah tashoof,	When I open the window you will see.
صحيح * حق	śa'hi'h, 'ha'k'k,	True.
الحق معك	al-'ha'k'k maعak,	You are right.
جيب لي ثيابي حالا * (بالعجل)	jib li thiâbi 'hâlan (bilعajal),	Bring me my clothes quickly.
اين هي * هيا فاين	aine hi, hia faine,	Where are they?
هناك علي الصندوق عند رأسك	honâc عala ssandoo'k عind râsak,	There, on the box' near your head.
رح الان وجيب لي مآ (مويه) حتي اغسل وجهي ويدي	ro'h alân wajib lî mâ (moyah) 'hatta agsil wajhi wa-yadiya,	Now go and bring me some water, that I may wash my face & hands.

ARABIC PARLANCE.	PRONUNCIATION.	ENGL. EQUIVALENTS.
تريده سخن	toridoh soćhn,	Do you want it warm?
لا ما انا بردان	lâ mâ anâ bardân,	No, I am not so cold.
اين الفوطه	aine alfoo'tah,	Where is the towel?
ما فيه فُوَط نظاف	mâ fih fowa't nithâf (nizâf),	There are no clean ones.
اعطيتهم للغساله	aعtytohom lilgassâlah,	I gave them to be washed.
نظـفـت تاسومتي (مركوبي)	nazzaft tâsoomati, (markoobi),	Have you cleaned my shoes?
لسّا ما نظفتها	lissâ mâ nazzafthâ,	As yet I have not cleaned them?
ولكن قبلما تلبس (تكون لبست) انظفها	wa-lâkin ćablamâ talbas (takoon labist) onazzifhâ,	But before you are dressed I will clean them.
نظفهم حالًا	nazzifhom 'hâlan,	Now clean them quickly.
امرك	amrać,	I obey your order.
جيب كرسي	gib corsî,	Bring a chair.
تفضل اقعد	tafaḋ́lal o'kعod,	Pray be seated.
ايش حالك ياسيدي	aish 'hâlać yâ sidi,	Well, Sir, how are you?

ARABIC PARLANCE.	PRONUNCIATION.	ENGL. EQUIVALENTS.
الحمد لله	al'hamdo lillâh,	Thanks.
تريد حاجه	torîd 'hâjah,	Do you want any thing ?
لا * كثر خيرك	lâ, cathir cheirak,	No, thank you.
مرادي من جنابك شي	morâdi min janâbac shy,	I have a request to make to you.
ايش هو	aish howa,	What is it ?
ان كان ما عندك شغل تعال معي الي البازار	in cân mâ عindak shogl taعal maعî ila lbâzâr,	If you have nothing to do, come with me to the bazaars.
نشتري بعض اشيآ	nashtari baعd ashyâ,	We will buy some things.
ايش مرادك تشتري	aish morâdac tashtarî,	What do you wish to buy ?
حاجات مختلفه	'hâjât moc'htalifah,	Different things.
من اي نوع	min eye nowع,	What kind ?
للاكل والشرب	lil acle wa shshorb,	To eat and to drink
احبّ ما عليّ	a'habb mâ عalyya,	Very well, with great pleasure.
نروح اذًا (امّال)	naroo'h ithan (ommâl),	Let us go, then.

ARABIC PARLANCE.	PRONUNCIATION.	ENGL. EQUIVALENTS.
ايش من فلوس عندك	aish min foloos ɛindac,	What kind of money have you?
ريالات	riyalât,	Dollars.
يصحّ	yaśi'h'h,	It will do.
خلّيني اشوف	ćhallîni ashoof,	Let me see.
هذا زغل	hâthâ zagal,	This one is false.
ايش نعمل	aish naɛmal,	What shall we do?
ما اعرف	mâ aɛrif,	I do not know.
خذ وانظر الباقي	ćhoth wanzor al-bá'ki,	Take and look at the rest.
دول طيّبين	dól 'tyibîn,	These are good.
خلّنا نروح صار وخري (تاخّرنا)	ćhalinâ naroo'h śâr waćhri (taaćhćharnâ),	Let us go, it is late.
ما بقي لنا وقت	mâ ba'ki lanâ wa'kt,	There is no more time.
لسّا فيه (مازال) وقت	lissa fîh (mâ zâl) wa'kt,	There is yet time.
قبلما يقفل البازار (يغلق) نصل	'kablamâ yoglać albazar na'sil,	Before the bazaar closes we will reach it.
نمشي بالعجل	namshi bilɛajal,	Let us walk quickly.
الساعه ثلاثه	assaɛah thalâthah,	Is it three o'clock?

THIRD DIALOGUE.

ARABIC PARLANCE.	PRONUNCIATION.	ENGL. EQUIVALENTS.
دا الوقت الاذان	dalwa′kt al-azan (al-athan),	They are now calling to prayers.
خلّنا نشوف في دي الدكّان	ćhallinâ nashoof fi di ddokkân,	Let us see in this shop.
مرحبا بكم ياخواجات ايش تنظروا	mar′haba bicom ya-ćhawâjât aish tanzoroo,	You are welcome, gentlemen. At what do you look?
عايزين سجادات صغيره	câyzîn sajjâdât ′sagîrah,	We want some small carpets.
شوف ما فيه احسن من دول	shoof mâ fih a′hsan min dôle,	See, there are none better than these.
طيب لكن قد ايش السعر	′tyib lâkin ′kadd-aish assiعr,	Good, but what is its price?
رخيص جدّا	ṛaćhî′s jiddan,	It is very cheap.
ايش * هو غالي	aish, howa gâli,	What! it is dear.
بقد ايش تعطيه	bi′kad aish taع′tih,	For how much will you give it?
قد ايش تعطي انت	′kadd aish taعti anta,	What do you offer?
خمسة وثلاثين قرش	ćhamsah wa thalâthin ćarsh (′kirsh)	Thirty-five piastres.

ARABIC PARLANCE.	PRONUNCIATION.	ENGL. EQUIVALENTS.
يا خواجات ما يمكن بانقص من خمسين ان اعجبكم	yâ ćhawâjât mâ yomkin bian'káś min ćhamsîn in aعjabcom,	Gentleman, not less than fifty, if you please.
ترید تاخذ اربعين	torîd taćhoth arbaعîn,	Will you take forty?
والّا خاطرك	wa illa ćhâ'tirak,	If not, adieu.
السعر دي يخسّرني	assiعr di yoćhassirni,	I shall lose by this price.
تربح (تكسب) من غيره	tarba'h (taksib), min ghyroh,	You will gain by something else.
اليوم ما بعت شي	al youm mâ biعt shy,	To-day I have sold nothing.
نعدّ الفلوس	naعodd al foloos,	Let us count the money.
علي التمام والكمال	عala ttamâm wa lcamâl,	Quite right.
انده ولد	indah walad,	Call a boy,
حتي ياخذها الي البيت	'hatta yaćhothhâ ila lbite,	that he may take it to the house.
خاطرك	ćhâ'tirak,	Good by.
في امان الله	fi amâni-illah,	With the peace of God.

FOURTH DIALOGUE.

ARABIC PARLANCE.	PRONUNCIATION.	ENGL. EQUIVALENTS.
جيب فطور	*jîb fo'toor,*	Bring breakfast.
جيب غدا	*jîb gadâ,*	Bring dinner.
جيب خبز	*jîb ćhobz,*	Bring bread.
جيب لبن	*jîb laban,*	Bring milk.
اعطِ سكر	*aعti soccar,*	Give sugar.
كل عشاك	*col عashâk,*	Eat your supper.
اشرب حليب	*ishrab 'halîb,*	Drink milk.
نور السراج	*nawir assirâj,*	Light the lamp.
نور الشمعه	*nawir ashshamعah*	Light the candle.
اطفي الشمعه	*a'tfi shshamعah,*	Put out the candle.
لا تنس	*la tansa,*	Do not forget.
تعال هنا	*taعâla honâ,*	Come here.
قرّب	*'carrib,*	Come near.
من اين جاَي	*min aine jâyi,*	Where do you come from ?
الي اين رايح	*ila aine râi'h,*	Where are you going ?
حَضّر الشاي	*'ha'd'dir ashshay,*	Make ready the tea.
مل الي اليمين	*mil ila al yamîn,*	Turn to the right.
مل الي الشمال	*mil ila ashshimâl,*	Turn to the left.
رح الي البيت حالا	*ro'h ila albite 'hâ-lan,*	Go home quickly.

ARABIC PARLANCE.	PRONUNCIATION.	ENGL. EQUIVALENTS.
انده للحمّالين	*indah al'hammâlin,*	Call the porters.
نحّ المائدة	*na'h'hi al mâidah,*	Take away the table.
احترص * احترس	*i'htaris,*	Be careful.
حضّر الكرّوسه	*'ha'd'dir al carroosah,*	Get ready the carriage.
انت فاضي	*anta fâ'di,*	Are you at leisure?
من كرمك سامحني	*min caramak sâmi'hni,*	Be pleased to forgive me.
عملت الفرشه	*amilt al farshah,*	Have you made the bed?
دربز الباب	*darbiz al bâb,*	Fasten the door.
هذي مصيبة	*hâthi mo'sîbah,*	This is a misfortune.
هم جهلا	*hom johalâ,*	They are ignorant.
جيب كتابي	*gib kitâbi,*	Bring my book.
رح الي السوق	*ro'h ila assoo'k,*	Go to the market.
جيب شوية لحم	*gib showyyat la'hm,*	Bring a little meat.

FIFTH DIALOGUE.

من نت	*man ant,*	Who are you?
لايش جيت	*leysh jeet,*	Why are you come?

ARABIC PARLANCE.	PRONUNCIATION.	ENGL. EQUIVALENTS.
تريد تقول لي شي	torid taćool li shy,	You will say something to me.
لاتكن ثقيل	la tacon tha'keal,	Don't be troublesome.
انا اخرج	ana achroj,	I will go out.
جيب ثيابي	gib thiábi,	Bring my clothes.
هم كلهم هناك	hom collohom honák,	They are all there.
من هو	man hoo,	Who is he?
هل احد هناك	hal a'had honák,	Is any one there?
قل دي كمان	'col di camân,	Say that again.
نحن نروح غدا	na'hn naroo'h gada,	We shall go tomorrow.
نح هذا	na'h'hi hâtha,	Move this way.
هذي فاكهه فاخره	hâthi fâkihah fâc'hirah,	This is a very fine fruit.
هذا خبر عجيب	hâtha 'chabar ɛajîb,	This is wonderful news.
نحن جوعانين وعطشانين	na'hn jouɛânin waɛa'tshânin,	We are hungry and thirsty.
هو رجل محترس (حريص)	howa rajol mo'htaris ('harî's),	He is a careful man.
هم كذابين كبار	hom caththâbin kibâr,	They are great liars.

G

ARABIC PARLANCE.	PRONUNCIATION.	ENGL. EQUIVALENTS.
قلبه محزون	'kalboh ma'hzoon,	His heart is grieved.
مصلحتك الان تمّت	ma'sla'hatak al-ân tammat,	Is your business now completed?
هل الدليل عليه قوى	hal addalil ₎alieh 'cawi,	Is the proof of it strong?
هي عديمة الفطنة	hia ₎adîmat alfi't-nah,	She is very impudent.
الجوّ صافي (صاحي)	al-jouw 'sâfi ('sâ-'hi),	The sky is quite clear.
دول اولاد يحبوا الاذية	dol owlâd yo'hib-bo al athiyah,	These are mischievous children.
كلهم بقوا مختفين	collohom ba'koo moc'htafîn,	They all remained hidden.
قلبه قلقان	'calboh 'cal'cân,	His heart is restless.
هو احمق	howa a'hma'k,	He is a fool.
هذا الورق مبلول	hâtha al wara'k mablool,	This paper is moist.
من عامل ضجة	man ₎âmil 'daj-jah,	Who is making a noise?
ايش عمال تقول	aish ₎ammâl ta-'kool,	What are you saying?

ARABIC PARLANCE.	PRONUNCIATION.	ENGL. EQUIVALENTS.
ايش اسم الرجل دي	aish ism arrajol di,	What is the name of this man?
هـل علي دكها الشجرة ثمر كثير	halعaladikha ash-shajarah tha-mar cathîr,	Is there much fruit on that tree?

SIXTH DIALOGUE.

نكلم بسهوله	tacallam bisohoo-luh,	Speak easy.
لا تعد تروح الي هناك	la taعod taroo'h ila honâk,	Go not there again.
من هو ساكن هناك	man hoo sâkin ho-nâk,	Who lives there?
جيب شوية نبيذ وماآ	gib sho-whyyat nabîth wa mâ,	Bring some wine and water.
بّرد المآء طيب	barrid almâ´ty-ib,	Cool the water well.
الغدآ علي المائدة	al gada عala al-mâ-idah,	The dinner is on the table.
ايش اسمك	aish ismak,	What is your name?
هو حاذق جدّا	howa 'hâthi'k jid-dan,	He is very clever.
صحيني بدري قوي	sa'h'hini badri ćawi,	Wake me very early.

G 2

ARABIC PARLANCE.	PRONUNCIATION.	ENGL. EQUIVALENTS.
اليوم صحو	al-youm śa'how,	It is fair to-day.
اعترف * اقرّ	ietaraf, a'karr,	He has made confession.
اصبر شويه	iśbir showhyyah,	Have patience a little.
ابعثهم الي بيتي	ibeathhom ila byti,	Send them to my house.
رش شوية مآ	roshsh showhyyat mâ,	Sprinkle a little water.
اقلب دكها الورقه	i'klib dikha al wara'kah,	Turn back that leaf.
اربط ايديهم وارجلهم	orbót aydihom wa-arjolhom,	Tie their hands and feet.
هنا فقير علي الباب	hona fa'kîr eala al bâb,	Here is a fakir at the door.
هو فهيم جدّا	howa fahîm jid-dan,	He is very intelligent.
دي عيش طيب قوي	di eeish´tyib ćawi,	This is very good bread.
ارجع في السكه دي	irjae fi assikhah di,	Come back this way.
خذ دكها المكتوب	ćhoth dikha al-maktoob,	Take this letter.

ARABIC PARLANCE.	PRONUNCIATION.	ENGL. EQUIVALENTS.
اخرج من البيت	*ochroj min al bite,*	Come out of the house.
اغسل يديك ووجهك	*igsil yadike wa-wajhak,*	Wash your hands and face.
عنده اصحاب كثير	*ʿindoh ásʿhâb ca-thîr,*	He has many friends.
ايش فائدة تكون في دكها	*aish fâ-idah ta-coon fi dikha,*	What benefit will there be in that?
كابدوا حزن كثير	*câbadoo 'hozn ca-thîr,*	They have suffered much sorrow.
له لحية طويله'	*loh li'hyah 'tawî-lah,*	He has got a long beard.
ايش من طير هذا	*aish min 'tire hâ-tha,*	What bird is this?
هو سكّير	*howa sikkir,*	He is a great drunkard.
حقل من هذا	*'ha'kl man hâtha,*	Whose field is this?
كم كان ناس هناك	*cam cân nâs ho-nâk,*	How many people were present?

SEVENTH DIALOGUE.

ما فيه زيت في السراج	*mâ fih zite fi assi-râj,*	There is no oil in the lamp.

ARABIC PARLANCE.	PRONUNCIATION.	ENGL. EQUIVALENTS.
اعطني من فضلك قلم	aعʹtini min faḋlac ʹkalam,	Pray give me a pen.
اين دكانه	aine dokkânoh,	Where is his shop?
الملك جلس علي السرير	al-malik jalas عa-la assarîr,	The king sat upon the throne.
صوته حسن	śoutoh ʹhasan,	His voice is good.
اي نوع حيوان هو هذا	eiye nouع ʹhaya-wân howa hâtha,	What sort of animal is this?
ايش نصيحتك * ما رايك	aish naʹsiʹhatak (ma rayak),	What is your advice?
قد ايش عمرك	ćadd aish عomrah,	What is your age?
كيف صحتك	keif siʹhʹhatak,	How is your health?
جيب حبر وقلم وورق	gib ʹhibr wa ćalam wa warák,	Bring ink, pen, and paper.
حصان من هذا	ʹhisân man hâtha,	Whose horse is that?
من هو دكها الافرنجي	man hoo dikha al-ifranji,	Who is that European?
هذه الارض بور	hathih al arḋ boor,	This soil is barren.
ايش شغل عمال تعمل	aish shogl عam-mâl taعmil,	What business are you doing?
عملوا اعذار كثيرة	عamalo aعthâr cathîrah,	They made much apology.

ARABIC PARLANCE.	PRONUNCIATION.	ENGL. EQUIVALENTS.
عندي وجع راس	؏indi waja؏ râs,	I have a headach.
صار وخري خلينا نتوجّه	'sar waćhri ćhal-lina nitwajjah,	It is late, let us depart.
يشتكي من وجع الكبد	yashtaki min wa-ja؏ al-cabid,	He has a liver complaint.
عنده وجع الضرس	؏indoh waja؏ a'ddirs,	He has a tooth-ache.
في البازار اشيا كثيرة للّعب	fi al-bazar ashya cathîrah lil-li؏b,	There are many playthings in the bazaar.
هذه الترجمة حسنة جدا	hâthih attarja-mah 'hasanah jiddan,	This translation is very good.
ساعتك تمشي طيب	sa؏atak tamshi 'ty-ib,	Your watch goes well.
دي شمع	di sham؏,	This is a wax can-dle.
كم كرا القارب	cam kira al'kârib,	How much is the fare of the boat?
كم الساعة	cam assâ؏ah,	What o'clock is it?
ارفع الستاير	irfa؏ assatâ-yer,	Lift up the blinds.
نحّ الصحون	na'h'hi aṡṡo'hoon,	Take away the dishes.

ARABIC PARLANCE.	PRONUNCIATION.	ENGL. EQUIVALENTS.
حطّ ساعتي علي المائدة	'ho'tt sâ‌ati ‌ala al-mâidah,	Place my watch on the table.
هذه الفاكهة حامضه	hathih al-fâkihah 'hâmi'dah,	This fruit is very acid.
لايش انت غضبان	laish anta ga'dbân,	Why are you angry?
دي شغل صعب قوي	di shogl sa‌b ćawi,	This is a very difficult business.
هم مكّارين قوي	hom makkârin ća-wi,	They are very artful.
القماش دي خشن قوي	al-ćomâsh di ćha-shin 'cawi,	This cloth is very coarse.
هل انت تصلح للشغل	hal anta taślo'h lishshogl,	Are you fit for the business?
اليوم ابرد من امس	al youm abrad min ams,	It is colder to-day than yesterday.
هي خرسا وطرشا	hia ćharsa wa-'tarsha,	She is dumb and deaf.
دي الحكايه كلها كذب	di al 'hicâyah col-loha kathib,	This story is all a lie.
هذا زبيب طيب	hâtha zabîb 'ty-ib,	These are fine raisins.
عنده بيت كبير	‌indoh bite cabîr,	He has a large house.

ARABIC PARLANCE.	PRONUNCIATION.	ENGL. EQUIVALENTS.
دي الاوضه شرحه قوي	di al-ou'dah shir-'hah ćawi,	This room is very well lighted.
دي الاوضه عاليه قوي	di al-oudah ćâli-yah ćawi,	This room is very lofty.
طبعه قاسي	'tabعoh ćâsi,	His disposition is cruel.
هم كسلانين ومتهاملين	hom caslânin wa-motahâmilin,	They are lazy and negligent.
دي القلم رخو بزياده	di al ćalam raćhow biziyâdah,	This pen is too soft.
هذا الورق خشن جدا	hâtha al wara'k c'hashin jiddan,	This paper is very coarse.
انت تتكلم بالتاني قوي	anta tatacallam bit-taanni ćawi,	You speak very slowly.
تقدر تتكلم بالانكليزي	ta'kdir tatacallam bilanklezi,	Can you speak English?
انزل والّا تقع	inzil wa-illa ta'kaع,	Descend, otherwise you will fall.
لابد انك تروح معي	la bodd annak ta-roo'h maعi,	You must go with me.
نحّ الحاجه دي	na'h'hi al-'hâjah di,	Take away this thing.
نعرفه كله	naعrifoh colloh,	We know it all.

ARABIC PARLANCE.	PRONUNCIATION.	ENGL. EQUIVALENTS.
يعرفوا كثير	ya‿rifo cathîr,	They know a great deal.
كلفني تعب كثير	callafni ta‿ab cathîr,	He gave me much trouble.
لايش تضحك بلا سبب	laish ta'd'hak bila sabab,	Why do you laugh without cause?
هذا ما هو بيتي	hâtha ma hoo byti,	This is not my house.
خليني اشم هذه الزهرة	'challini ashomm hâthih azzahrah,	Allow me to smell that flower.
ادهن الكرسي بالزيت	idhan al corsi bizzile,	Apply oil to the chair.
افتح الباب	ifta'h al-bâb,	Open the door.
بعض من العساكر انجرحوا	ba‿'d min al‿asâkir injara'ho,	Some of the soldiers have been wounded.
اضرب دكها الولد الكسلان	i'drib dika al walad al caslân,	Beat that lazy boy.
بعد ان قال هذا سافر (انطلق)	ba‿d an câl hâtha sâfar (in'tala'k),	Having said this, he departed.
كم بلغت قائمة حسابك	cam balagat 'kâimat 'hisâbak,	What is the amount of your bill?

ARABIC PARLANCE.	PRONUNCIATION.	ENGL. EQUIVALENTS.
ايش هو الفرق بين دول الاثنين	eish hoo al far'k bine dol al ith-nine,	What is the difference between these two ?
كما هو المعلم كذلك يكون المتعلم	cama hoo al moₑallim cathâlik yacoon al-motaₑallim,	As the master, so will be the scholar.

EIGHTH DIALOGUE.

كم من فصل في هذا الكتاب	cam min faśl fi hâtha al kitâb,	In this book how many chapters are there ?
هل علي هذه البضاعة اسقاط في الحساب	halₑala hâthih al-bi'dâₑah is'kâ't fi al'hisâb,	On these goods is there any discount ?
هذا الصبي محبّب الينا جدا	hâtha assabi mo-'habbab ilyna jiddan,	This boy is much loved by us.
هل في هذا الغدير سمك	hal fi hâtha al ga-dîr samak,	In this tank are there any fish ?
اصطدت سمكة بعصا	is'tatt samacah bi-ₑaśa,	I caught a fish with a rod.
هذه البقرة ما لها قرون	hâthih al ba'karah ma laha 'koroon,	This cow has no horns.

ARABIC PARLANCE.	PRONUNCIATION.	ENGL. EQUIVALENTS.
من اي نوع هذا الجوخ	min eye nouع hâtha al jooĉh,	Of what kind is this cloth ?
هل في نيتك ان تسافر الي اوربا	hal fi niyatak an tosâfir ila ourobba,	Do you intend going to Europe ?
علّق هذه الثريا (النجفة) في القاعه	عalli´k hâthih aththoryia (annagafah) fi al-´kâعah,	Hang up this lamp in the hall.
هل تسافر في البرّاو في البحر	hal tosâfir fi al-barrow fi al ba´hr,	Do you go by land or by water ?
صندوقك ما له قفل	sandou´kak ma la-ho (loh) ´kofl,	There is no lock to your box.
علي طرف النهر وحل كثير	عala´taraf annahr wa´hl kathîr,	There is much mud on the river side.
كم كان من المسافرين في ذلك المركب	cam cân min al-mosâfirin fi thâlik al markab,	How many passengers were in that vessel ?
تعطر البيت كله	taعa´ttar al bite colloh,	The whole room was scented.
هل انت صاحب هذه الدار	hal anta sâ´hib hâthih addâr,	Are you the owner of this house ?

ARABIC PARLANCE.	PRONUNCIATION.	ENGL. EQUIVALENTS.
كما تفعل كذلك تلاقي	*cama tafɛal kathâlik tolâ'ki,*	Such as you will do, so will you find.
التسليم خير رفيق	*attaslim éhire rafî'k,*	Resignation is the best companion.
الدنيا دار غرور	*addonya dâr gorour,*	The world is the house of deceit.
ثمرة التهوّر (العجلة) الندامة	*thamarat attahawor (alɛajalah) annadâmah,*	The fruit of rashness is repentance.
الصبر منقبة محمودة	*a'ssabr man'kabah ma'hmoodah,*	Patience is an excellent quality.
السماع خير من الكلام	*assamâɛ c'hire min al calâm,*	Hearing is better than speaking.
كما تتكلم كذلك تسمع	*cama tatacallam cathâlik tasmaɛ,*	Such as you speak, so will you hear.
القناعة مفتاح الراحة	*al-'kanâɛah miftâ'h arrâ'hah,*	Contentment is the key of repose.
الجهل موت الاحياء	*al jahl mout al-a'hyâ,*	To be ignorant is death to the living.
الاقتصاد في كل شي خير	*al-i'ktiśâd fi coll shy c'hire,*	Moderation in every thing is best.

ARABIC PARLANCE.	PRONUNCIATION.	ENGL. EQUIVALENTS.
لحكيم تكفيه اشارة	al-'hakîm takfih al-ishârah,	To the wise a hint is enough.
ساعد اخاك في الشدة	sâعid aćhâk fi ash-shiddah,	Assist your brother in distress.
الدوآ كثيرا ما يكون دآ	addawâ cathîran ma yacoon dâ,	Very frequently medicine is sickness.
الانسان يعرف بسيرته	al-insân yoعraf bisîratoh,	Man becomes known from his conduct.
من المنع تزيد الرغبة	min al-manعtazîd arragbah,	From prohibition desire increases.
البخت لا ياتي مع لحكمة	al-baćht la yâti maعal-'hikmah,	Fortune does not come with wisdom.

NINTH DIALOGUE.

في مدة هذا الشهر وقع مطر كثير	fi moddat hâtha ashshahr waʻkaع maʻtar cathîr,	During this month much rain fell.
ابعث خادما الي هناك	ibعath ćhâdim ila honâk,	Send a servant there.
اقعد تحت هذه الشجرة	oʻkعod taʻht hâthih ashshajarah,	Sit under this tree.

ARABIC PARLANCE.	PRONUNCIATION.	ENGL. EQUIVALENTS.
كم ثمن هذه اللالي	cam thaman hâ-thih al-la-âli,	What is the price of these pearls?
ما اعظم (ما يكون) ثقل هذا الحجر	ma aعtham (ma yacoon) tho'kl hâtha al-'hajar,	How heavy will this stone be?
ايش اسم هذه القرية	eish ism hâthih al-'karyah,	What is the name of this village?
جيب حصان الركوب	jib 'hiŝân arro-koob,	Bring the riding horse.
انفض الستارات طيب حتي لا يبقي فيها ناموس (برغش)	onfo'd assitârât 'tyib 'hatta la yab'ka fiha bar-gash,	Brush the curtains well, so that no mosquito may remain.
يحب ان نكون محسنين	yajib an nakoon mo'hsinîn,	We ought to be benevolent.
وقعنا في صعوبات عظيمة	wa'kaعna fi soعo-bât عazîmah,	We have fallen in-to great difficul-ties.
كثير من المراكب تعطلت من النو	cathîr min al-ma-râkib taعa'tta-lat min annow,	Many ships have been damaged by the storm.
هو يشرب في كل يوم اللبن الطري	howa yashrab fi coll youm al-laban a'ttari,	He every day drinks new milk.

ARABIC PARLANCE.	PRONUNCIATION.	ENGL. EQUIVALENTS.
القعود مع السكوت خير من النزاع	al-'koعod maع as-socoot ćhire min annizâع,	To sit still is better than quarrelling.
اطحن هذا القمح بالرحي	i'than hâtha al-'kam'h birra'ha,	Grind this wheat in the mill.
تعرف وكيله مَن هو	taعrif wakîloh man howa (hoo),	Do you know who is his agent?
اشترِلي شمعدانين	ishtari li shamعa-dânine,	Buy two candlesticks for me.
هذا القطّ له اظافر كبيرة	hâtha al-'ki'tt la-ho (loh) azâfir cabîrah,	This cat has large claws.
خذ هذا الكرسي الي الاوضة الاخري	ćhoth hâtha al-corsi ila al-ou-'dat al-oćhra,	Take away this chair into the other room.
انا اريك صورة جميله	ana orîk śoorah jamîlah,	I will shew you a beautiful picture.
امضاؤك لا بد منه علي هذا العقد	im'dâk la 'bodd minho (minh) عala hâtha al-عa'kd,	Your signature is necessary to this bond.
اليوم يكون ضيف في دارهم	al-youm yacoon 'difi fi dârihom,	To-day there is a guest in their house.

ARABIC PARLANCE.	PRONUNCIATION.	ENGL. EQUIVALENTS.
صار وخري كثير	sâr wachri cathîr,	It is very late.
اسمح لنا بان نروح الي البيت	isma'h lana bi an naroo'h ila al-bite,	Permit us to go home.
في هذا الامر قساوة زائدة	fi hâtha al-amr 'kasâwah zâ-idah,	In this affair there is much cruelty.
قدامنا سفرة طويلة	'hoddâmana saf-rah 'tawîlah,	We have at pre-sent a long jour-ney.
الانسان له عقل اما البهيمة فلا	al-insân laho ع a'kl amma al-bahî-mah fala,	Man has reason, a brute none.
من فضلك اعطني كتاب توصية	min fa'dlak a ع tini kitâb tou'siyah,	Please give me a letter of intro-duction.
لايش تكتب بقلم ردي	leish taktob bi'ka-lam radi,	Why do you write with a bad pen ?
اي هذين الاثنين احسن	eye hâthine al-ith-nine a'hsan,	Of these two, which is the best ?
انا آخذ الشغل من يدك واعطيه اياه	ana âchoth ash-shogl min yadak wa-o ع 'tih iyâh,	I will take the business from you and give it to him.

ARABIC PARLANCE.	PRONUNCIATION.	ENGL. EQUIVALENTS.
ذهابك الي هناك غير لازم	thahâbak ila honâk gire lâzim,	Your going there is not necessary.
هو خبير بالعلم جدّا	howa ćhabîr bil-ilmع jiddan,	He is well versed in science.
هو عالم جدّا	howa ćâlim jiddan,	He is very learned.
هذا يكون احسن الجميع	hâtha yacoon a'h-san al-jamîعع,	This will be best of all.
قل لي ما يقول	'kol li ma ya'kool,	Tell me what he is saying.
قل للسائس يحضر للحصان	'kol lissâ-is yo-'ha'd'dir al 'hi-sân,	Tell the groom to get the horse ready.

TENTH DIALOGUE.

انا كذلك اريد ان اخرج	ana cathâlik orîd an aćhroj,	I also wish to go out.
لايش تصعد الي هذه الشجرة	leish ta'صعad ila hâthih ashsha-jarah,	Why do you climb this tree?
متي تكون قادرا علي السفر	mata tacoon 'kâ-dir عala assafar,	When will you be able to depart.
هل السرج علي الحصان او لا	hal assarj عala al-'hi'sân ow la,	Is the saddle on the horse or not?

ARABIC PARLANCE.	PRONUNCIATION.	ENGL. EQUIVALENTS.
نحن نرجع بعد دقائق	na'hn narjaع baعd da'kâye'k,	We will return in a few minutes.
ان كان الغدآ حاضرا جيبه (جيبه)	in cân al gadâ 'hâdir jiboh,	If dinner is ready bring it.
هل تعرف هذا الرجل	hal taعrif hâtha arrajol,	Do you know this man?
حصّل من العلم كثيرا	'ha'ssal min al-عilm cathîr,	He has acquired much science.
جمع ثروة جزيلة	jamaع tharwah jazîlah,	He has amassed much wealth.
تعال خلّنا نحن الاثنين نتحدت شويّة	taعâla éhallina na'hn al-ithnine nata'haddath showy-yah,	Come, let us two have some talk.
هل حصان واحد يقدر على جرّ ثقل مثل هذا	hal 'hisân wâ'hid ya'kdir عala jarr tho'hl mithl hâtha,	Will one horse be able to draw so great a weight?
تقدم انت نحن نجي	ta'kaddam anta na'hn naji,	You go on, we are coming.
هذه الحاجات جات من اوربا	hathih al-'hajât jâat min orobba,	These things are come from Europe
اين نقفي هذه الليلة	eine na'k di hâthih al-lylah,	Where shall we pass the night?

H 2

ARABIC PARLANCE.	PRONUNCIATION.	ENGL. EQUIVALENTS.
ما عندنا الان وقت للّعب	ma ⲅindana al-ân waˊkt lilliⲅb,	We have no time to play at present.
احرق رجله بالماء السخن	aˊhraˊk rigloh bil-mâ assoⲅhn,	He has scalded his foot.
هذه السكاكين كلها صدي	hâthih assakâkin colloha ˊsada,	All these knives are rusty.
هولآ الاولاد يصرخون طول النهار	hâ-oulâ al-aulâd yoˊsarriⲅhoˊtool annahâr,	These children are screaming all day.
كنا نفتّش علي هذا طول النهار	conna nofattish ⲅala hâthaˊtool annahâr,	We were seeking for this all day.
هل ختمت مكتوبك	hal ⲅhatamt mak-toobak,	Have you sealed your letter?
بيتنا مظلل بالشجر	biteana mozallal bishshajar,	Our house is shaded with trees.
عمال تمطر خلينا نتآوي عندك	ⲅammal tamˊtor ⲅhallina nit-âwa ⲅindak,	It is raining, give us shelter.
تقدّم الي هناك وقف	taˊkaddam ila ho-nâk waˊkif,	Go forward there, and stand still.
اخرج هذه الحاجات من الصندوق	aⲅhrij hâthih al-ˊhâjât min aˊs-sandooˊk,	Bring out these things from the box.

ARABIC PARLANCE.	PRONUNCIATION.	ENGL. EQUIVALENTS.
تكلّم بالعالي حينئذ اسمعك	tacallam bil عâli ´hînaïthin asma عak,	Speak loud, then I shall hear you.
ايش اسم دي بالعربي	eish ism di bil عarabi,	What do you call that in Arabic?
وافقني هذا المرة	wâfa´kani hâthih al marrah,	He agreed with me this time.
تدرّب نفسك في الكتابة والقرآة	todarrib nafsak fi al-kitâbah wal-´kirâ-ah,	You exercise yourself in writing and reading.
عند سماعهم هذا الخبر حصل لهم رعب شديد	عind samâ عihom hâtha al chabar ha´sal lahom ro عb shadîd,	On hearing this news they were much frightened.
كم يسع هذا الصندوق من النيله (النيل)	cam yasa ع hâtha as´sandoo´k min annîl,	How much indigo will this chest contain?
كلهم اغتاظوا من بعضهم بعض	collohom igtâzoo min ba ع´dihom ba عd,	They are all offended with one another.
نجونا من يد العدو	najouna min yad al- عadoo,	We have escaped from the hand of the enemy.
المدينة باسرها غرقت بالماء	al-madînah biasriha gari´kat bil mâ,	The whole city has been flooded.

ARABIC PARLANCE.	PRONUNCIATION.	ENGL. EQUIVALENTS.
بهذا يزداد فرحنا	*bihâtha yazdâd fa-ra'hna,*	With this our joy will be increased.
قللّنا مصروفنا للغاية	*'kallana ma'sroo-fana lilgâ-yah,*	We have much reduced our expenditure.
هذه الدراهم لازم انها ترجع اليه	*hâthih addarâhim lâzim annaha tarjaɛ ilyh,*	This money must be sent back to him.
سطّر ورقك ثم اكتب	*sa'ttir wara'kak thomma octob,*	Rule your paper, then write.
القوم كلهم ماتوا من الجوع	*al-'koum collohom mâtoo min al-jooɛ,*	All the people have died with hunger.
وقع بعضهم علي بعض	*wa'kaɛ baɛ'dohom ɛala baɛ'd,*	They have fallen one upon another.
يعيشون عيشا نكدا	*yaɛishoon ɛiesh nakid,*	They live in great affliction.
بني بيتا علي شاطي النهر	*bana bite ɛala shâ'ti annahr,*	He has built a house on the bank of the river.

ELEVENTH DIALOGUE.

ARABIC PARLANCE.	PRONUNCIATION.	ENGL. EQUIVALENTS.
علیمَ نهرب لیس ههنا خطر	ɛala ma nahrob lise hahona (ma fih hona) ćha-'tar,	Why should we run away? there is no danger here.
هجر اصدقآه	hajar aśdi'kâh,	He has abandoned his friends.
ساروا الي بلاد الافرنج من ستة اشهر	sâroo ila bilâd al-ifranj min sittat ashhor,	They went to Europe six months ago.
عند سماعهم تقريرا من هذا القبيل صاروا يضحكون	ɛind samâɛihom ta'krir min hâtha al-'kabîl sâroo yaɖ'hakoo,	On hearing a statement of this sort they began to laugh.
تعب في تعليمنا تعبا عظيما	taɛib fi taɛlimina taɛab ɛazîm,	He has taught us with great labour.
وجدنا برحمة الله راحة	wajadna bira'hmat allah ra'hah,	By the grace of God we have found repose.
اليوم مغيوم فيحتمل انها تمطر كثيرا	alyoum magyoum fa-ya'htamil an-naha tam'tor cathîr,	It is very cloudy, perhaps it will rain much.

ARABIC PARLANCE.	PRONUNCIATION.	ENGL. EQUIVALENTS.
في هذه الدار قاعة وثلثة بيوت (اوض)	fi hâthih addâr 'kâ3ah wa thalâthat boyout (owa'd),	In this house there is a hall and three rooms.
منذ كم بلغك هذا الخبر	month cam balagak hâtha al-ćhabar,	How long is it since you received this news?
بكم تبيع هذا لسيدي	bikam tabi3 hâtha li sidi,	For how much will you sell this to my master?
ابق هنا حتي نرجع	ib'ka hona 'hatta narja3,	Remain here until we return.
وقع السكين من يدي في النهر	wa'ka3 assikkin min yadi fi an-nahr,	The knife fell from my hand into the river.
الانسان الذي لا يقدر يتكلم بلغة القوم الذين يسكن بينهم قد يموت من الجوع	al-insân allathi (il-li) la ya'kdir yatacallam bi-logat al-'koum allathin yaskon bynahom 'kad yamoot min al-joo3,	A man who cannot speak the language of the people among whom he sojourns may sometimes be in danger of starving.

ARABIC PARLANCE.	PRONUNCIATION.	ENGL. EQUIVALENTS.
حضر الفطور	haḍḍir al-fo'toor,	Get the breakfast ready.
اشو شوية خبز وضع (حط) عليه زبده	ishwi showhy-yat ćhobz wa 'ho'tt ɛalieh zobdah,	Toast some bread, and butter it.
هل المآ يغلي	hal al mâ yagli,	Does the water boil?
اعط الخواجه فنجان شاي أخر	aɛ'ti al-ćhawâjah finjân shây â-ćhar,	Give the gentleman another cup of tea.
اعمله قوي بالكفاية واذا وضعت فيه حليب كثير وسكر يجي دائما طيب بحيث يكون الما يغلي	aɛ miloh 'kawi bil-kifâyah wa itha wa'daɛt fih ha-lib kathîr wasok-kar yaji dâiman 'ty-ib bi'hithe yacoon al-mâ yagli,	Make it strong enough; and putting in it plenty of milk and sugar you will always make it good, provided the water be actually boiling.
اعطني فنجان قهوه وشوية سكر كمان	aɛtini finjân 'kah-wah wa-sho-why-yat sokkar camân,	Give me a cup of coffee, and a little more sugar.
اسلق بيض ولكن لا تخليه ييبس	isli'k bi'de wa lâkin la tóćhallih ye-bas,	Boil some eggs, but do not let them get hard.

ARABIC PARLANCE.	PRONUNCIATION.	ENGL. EQUIVALENTS.
هات خبز وحلويات وكعك	hât chobz wa'holwiyât wakaعk,	Bring bread, sweetmeats, and cakes.
انت تعرف اني ما اقدر اشرب شاي من غير حليب	anta (ant) taعrif anni ma a'kdir ashrab shây min gire 'halib,	You know I cannot drink tea without cream.
الخبز ردي ملآن من الرمل	al-chobz radi malân min arraml,	The bread is bad, and full of sand.
المآ الذي عمل به هذا الشاي ما كان يغلي	almâ allathi inعamamal bih hâtha ashshây ma cân yagli,	The water with which this tea is made has not been boiling.
ما له طعم اصلا	ma loh 'taعm a'slan,	It has no taste at all.
قل للطباخ يحضر الغدا في الساعة الثالثة	'kol li'ttabbâch yo'haddir al gada fi assâعah ath-thâlithah,	Tell the cook to have the dinner ready at three o'clock.
ياسيدي الغدا حاضر	yâ-sidi algada'hâ-'dir,	Sir, dinner is ready.
اين الشوربة وملعقة الشوربة	aine ashshourabah wa-milعa'kat ashshourabah,	Where is the soup, and the soup spoon?

ARABIC PARLANCE.	PRONUNCIATION.	ENGL. EQUIVALENTS.
جيب شوية عيش وبطاطس وخضرة زي الهليون والملفوف والقرنبيط واللفت والجزر والخيار	jib showyyat ᶜiesh wa-batâtis wa-ĉho'drah zy al-halyoon wal mal-foof wal 'karna-bi't wal-lift wal-jazar wal-ĉhi-yâr,	Bring some bread, potatoes, greens, asparagus, cabbage, cauliflowers, turnips, carrots, and cucumbers.
جيب لحم بقر وضأن وعجل وسمك وفراخ ودجاج	jib la'hm ba'kar wa 'dân wa-ᶜigl wa-samak wa-firaĉh wa-dajâj,	Bring some beef, mutton, veal, fish, fowl, and venison.
غدا نتغدي في الريف ابعث كل شي في وقته	gada natagodda fi arrif ibᶜath coll shy fi wa'ktoh,	To-morrow we shall dine in the country: send every thing in time.
الان يمكنكم كلكم ان تنطلقوا معكم اذن	alân yomkinkom collokom an tan-'tali'hoo, maᶜ-kom ithn,	Now you may all depart, you have leave.
قل لي اسم هذا بلغتكم	'kol li ism hâtha bilogatkom,	Tell me the name of this in your own language.

GOAL—H

ARABIC PARLANCE.	PRONUNCIATION.	ENGL. EQUIVALENTS.
لا تقل لاحد الذي قلته لك بخصوص ذلك الكتاب	la ta´kol lia´had allathi ´koltoh lak bićhoŝooś thâlik al kitâb,	Do not tell any one what I said to you about that book.
قل له يجي هنا	´kol loh yaji hona,	Bid him come here.
قل له انه خبيث كبير	´kol loh ınnoh ćhabîth kabîr,	Tell him he is a great rogue.
خذني الي للخواجه فلان	ćhothni ila al-ćhawâjah folân,	Take me to Mr. B.
انت تهت عن الطريق الي بيته	ant niht Ɛan a´ttarî´k ila bytoh,	You have lost the road to his house?
ما معي فلوس ولكن اذا تبعتني تاخذ فلوسك في بيتي	ma maƐı foloos wa lâkin itha tabiƐtani ta´choth foloosak fi byti,	I have no cash about me, but if you will follow me you will receive your money at my house.
هل تتكلم بلساننا	hal tatacallam bilisânina,	Do you speak our language?
نعم ياسيدي انا اتكلم بالعربي قليلا	naƐam yâ-sidi ana atacallam bilƐarabi ´kalîl,	Yes, Sir, I can speak a little Arabic.

ARABIC PARLANCE.	PRONUNCIATION.	ENGL. EQUIVALENTS.
قد ايش لك في هذه البلاد	'kad aish lak fi hâ-thih al-bilâd,	How long have you been in this country ?
سنتين * عامين	sanatine, عâmine,	Two years.
امكث عندي ايّاما قليلة	omcoth عindi ey-yâm 'kalîlah, (cam youm),	Abide with me a few days.
عنده اهلية عظيمة	عindoh ahliyah عa-zimah,	He possesses great ability.
هو رجل قادر	howa rajol 'kâdir,	He is an able man.
لك مقدرة علي فعل هذا	lak ma'kdarah عa-la fiعl hâtha,	Are you able to do this ?
كنت غائبا عشرة ايام	cont gâ-ib عasha-rat ey-yâm,	I have been absent ten days.
يجب ان نتجنب فعل الشر	yajib an natajan-nab fiعl ash-sharr,	We ought to ab-stain from com-mitting evil.
الكلام هكذا فارغ (ضد المعقول)	al-kalâm hâkathu fârigh ('didd al-maع'kool),	It is absurd to speak thus.
خذ قدر ما يعجبك عندي كثير	choth 'kadr ma yoعjibak عindi cathîr,	Take as much as you please, I have abundance.

ARABIC PARLANCE.	PRONUNCIATION.	ENGL. EQUIVALENTS.
هل رضيت بما عرضت عليك اولا	hal raḍit bima ʿaraʾdt ʿalike oue la,	Do you accede to what I have proposed, or not?
الكتاب الذي بعثت لي حاز القبول	al-kitâb allathi baʿatht li ʾhâz al-ʾkabool,	The book you sent me was acceptable.
ان لم ترافقني لا اروح	in lam torâfiʿkni la aroo'h,	Except you accompany me, I will not go.
ما قدرت ان ابلغ (اتمم) مرادي	ma ʾkadart an ablogh (otammim) morâdi,	I was not able to accomplish my wishes.
هل عندك معه حساب	hal ʿindak maʿoh ʾhisâb,	Have you an account with him?
اشتكي عليه انه سرق معلمه	oshtoki ʿalihe an-noh saraʾk moʿallimoh,	He is accused of robbing his master.
عوّد نفسك علي القرآة والكتابة	ʿawid nafsak ʿala al'kirâ-ah wal-kitâbah,	Accustom yourself to read and write.
هذه الفاكهة حامضة جدا	hâthih al-fâkihah hâmidah jiddan,	This fruit is very acid.
عنده معارف كثيرة	ʿindoh maʿârif cathîrah,	He has many acquaintances.

ARABIC PARLANCE.	PRONUNCIATION.	ENGL. EQUIVALENTS.
حصّل معارف جزيله	'hassal maɛârif jazîluh,	He has acquired great knowledge.
الـفـعـل الطيب جدير بالثنآ منا	al-fiɛl a'tty-ib ja-dîr biththanâ minna,	A good action de-serves our praise.
هو مجدّ جدا في ذلك الامر (الشغل)	ho mojidd jiddan fi thâlik al-amr (ashshogl),	He is exceedingly active in that business.
زادت جمكيته	zâdat jamkiyatoh,	He has received an addition to his salary.
هذا خطّ يعجب	hâtha ćha'tt yoɛ-jib,	This is admirable writing.
اتعجب منه لوفور علمه	ataɛajjab minh li-wofoor ɛilmoh,	I admire him for his great learn-ing.
لا اسلّم بما تقول	la osallim bima ta'kool,	I do not admit of what you say.
تقدر تسلفني هذا المبلغ	ta'kdir toslifni hâ-tha al-mablagh,	Can you advance me this sum?
العدوّ تقدم حتي الي —	al-ɛadoo ta'kad-dam 'hatta ila —,	The enemy has advanced as far as ——

ARABIC PARLANCE.	PRONUNCIATION.	ENGL. EQUIVALENTS.
اي فائدة يكون لي من هذا	eye fâ-idah yacoon li min hâtha,	Of what advantage will that be to me?
صارلها زمان طويل في الضيق	sâr laha zamân 'tawîl fi ađ'di'k,	She has long been in adversity.
ما رايك (نصيحتك) في هذا الامر	ma râyak (na-śi'hatak) fi hâ-tha al-amr,	What is your advice in this affair?
تكلّف لان اظهر معروفا كثيرا	takallaf li-an az-har maعroof ka-thîr,	He affected a great show of kindness.
هذا القصة موثرة (فعّالة * بالغة)	hâthih al-'kiśśah moaththirah (faعâlah, bâligah),	This history is affecting.
يظهر للناس مودة جزيله	yozhir linnâs ma-waddah jazîlah,	He shows great affection for the people.
انا اخاف من التوجه الي هناك	ana aćhâf min at-tawajjoh ila ho-nâk,	I am afraid to go there.
ما اريد ان اجبهه (اكسفه)	ma orid an ajla-hoh (aksifoh),	I do not wish to affront him.

ARABIC PARLANCE.	PRONUNCIATION.	ENGL. EQUIVALENTS.
سنّها ما هو اكثر من عشر سنين	sinnaha mâ ho akthar min ɛashr sinîn,	Her age is not more than ten years.
تعرف شيخه من هو	taɛrif sheićhoh man ho,	Do you know who is his tutor?
اوافقك علي ما تقول	owâfi'kak ɛala mâ ta'kool,	I agree to what you say.
ايّ اتفاق كان بينك وبينه	eye ittifâ'k cân bynak wa-bynoh,	What agreement had you with him?
اي تغيير (تبديل) اعمل	eye tagyeer (tabdîl) aɛmal,	What alteration shall I make?
تلّه (تسلّ) في هذا البستان قليلا	talahha (tasalla) fi hâtha al bostân 'kalîl,	Amuse yourself a while in the garden.
هذه مدينة قديمة (عتيقة)	hâthih madînah 'kadîmah (ɛatî'kah),	This is an ancient city.
هل يغضبك هذا	hal yog'dibak hâtha,	Does this make you angry?
تعرف اسم هذا الحيوان	taɛrif ism hâtha al-'hayawân,	Do you know this animal's name?

I

ARABIC PARLANCE.	PRONUNCIATION.	ENGL. EQUIVALENTS.
تقدر تعطيني جواب هذه المسئله	ta'kdir to'tini jawâb hâthih almas-alah,	Can you give me an answer to this question?
انا في قلق حتي اذهب الي هناك	ana fi' kala'k' hatta athhab ila honâk,	I am anxious to get there.
ما اعتذر عن سلوكه	ma i'tathar 'an solokoh,	He made no apology for his misconduct.
يظهرلي انه غريب	yathhar li annoh garîb,	It appears to me very strange.
هل تستصوب ما اقول	hal tasta'swib ma a'kool,	Do you approve of what I say?
يورد دلائل قوية	yourid dalâil 'kawiyah,	He uses very strong arguments.
هل سمعت بقدومه	hal sami't bi'kodoo'moh,	Have you heard of his arrival?
الملك كان علي راس جيشه	al-malik cân 'ala râs jyshoh,	The king was at the head of his army.
ما لي خبرة بذلك الفن	mâ li 'hibrah bi-thâlik al-fann,	I am not acquainted with that art.

ARABIC PARLANCE.	PRONUNCIATION.	ENGL. EQUIVALENTS.
هم محتالون	hom mo'htâloon,	They are very art-ful.
يتعاطون اصنافا مختلفة	yataعa'toon aśnâf moćhtalifah,	They deal in va-rious articles.
خلنا الان نطلع الي الجبل	ćhallina al-ân na't-laع ila al jabal,	Let us now ascend the mountain.
اهل القرية اجتمعوا	ahl al-'kar-yah ij-tamaعoo,	The people of the village assem-bled.
رايت جاعة عظيمة من الناس	raeyt (shoft) ja-mâعah عazimah min annâs,	I saw a great as-sembly of peo-ple.
قبلتُ بمعروضك	'kabilt bi-maعroo-'dak,	I assent to your proposal.
زعم انه كذلك	zaعam annoh ca-thâlik,	He asserted that it is so.
يجب ان نساعد بعضنا بعضا	yajib an nosâعid baعdna baعdan,	We ought to assist each other.
لماذا تعاشر الرفقة الاشرار	limâtha toعâshir arrifćah al-ash-râr,	Why do you asso-ciate with evil company?
احقق لك انه ليس في هذا الامرخطر	o'ha'kki'k lak an-noh lise fi hâtha al-amr éha'tar,	I assure you there is no danger in that matter.

ARABIC PARLANCE.	PRONUNCIATION.	ENGL. EQUIVALENTS.
خيالة العدوّ اقتحمونا	ćhiyâlat al-ɛadou i'kta'hamouna,	The enemy's cavalry attacked us.
خلّنا نواظب علي فرضنا	ćhallina nowâthib ɛala far'dina,	Let us attend to our duties.
هي منعكفة علي العلم	hia monɛakifah ɛala al ɛilm,	She pays attention to learning.

VOCABULARY.

v. stands for verb.

s. . . . . substantive.

pr. . . . . pronounced.

A.

Ability, مقدرة * استطاعة ma'k-darah, isti'taᵉah

Able, قادر 'kâdir

Above, فوق fou'k

Absence, غياب giyâb

Absent, غائب gâib

Absurd, غيرالحق * محال mohâl, gair al'ha'k'k

Abundance, كثرة cathrah

Accept, قبول ćabool

Accommodate, تيسير tyseer

Accomplish, اتمام itmâm

Accustomed, تعوّد taᵉou-ad

Acid, حامض hâmi'd

Acquaintance, معرفة maᵉri-fah

Acquainted, عارف * مطلّع علي mottalliᵉ ala, ćârif

Action, فعل fiᵉl

Active, مجدّ * عمول ᵉamool, mogidd

Add, v. اضاف a'dâf

Admirable, رائع * معجب mo-gib, râiᵉ

Advantage, فائدة fâidah

Advantageous, نافع * مفيد mo-feed, nâfiᵉ

Advice, نصيحة na'si'hah

Advise (to give notice), اخبار ićhbâr

Affection, مودة mawaddah

Affectionate, ودود wadood

Afraid (to be), خائف ćhâif

Again, ايضا * كذلك cathâlik,
ey'dan

Against, علي * ضّد ṣala,'didd

Age, عمر * سّن sinn, ṣomr

Agree, اتفق ittafa'k

Agreeable, موافق * مشتهي
moshtaha, mowâfi'k

Agreement, شرط shar't

Aid, مساعده mosâ ṣadah

Air, هوآ hawâ

Alive, حّي 'hye

Allow (to let), اذن * اجازه ija-
thah, ithn

Alter (to), غير gyeyar

Amuse, تلّهي * تسّلي talahha,
tasalla

Amusement, لَهْو lahow

Ancient (old), قديم * عتيق
'kadeem, ṣatee'k

Answer, v. جاوب jâwab

Answer, s. جواب jawâb

Anxious, قَلق 'kali'k

Approve, v. استصوب ista'swab

Arise, قام ṣâm

Army, عسكر ṣaskar

Arrival, قدوم * وصول wo'sool,
ćodoom

Art (trade), حرفة * صنعة san-
ṣah, 'hirfah

Artful, محارف * داهي mo-
'hârif, dâhi

Ask, v. سأل sa-al

Assemble, v. جمع jamaṣ

Assist, اعان عع-ân

Assure, v. اكّد accad

Astonish, v. عجّب ṣajjab

Attack, v. هجم hajam

Attention, انتباه * احتراس in-
tibâh, i'htirâs

Attentive, منتبه montabih

Authority, سلطان * سلطة sol-
'tah, sol'tân

Avoid, v. تجنب tajannob

Awake, v. استيقظ isty'kaz

B.

Back, ظهر zahr

Bad, ردي radi

Bag, كيس kees

Baggage, اثقال athćâl

Bargain, مساومه * شرية mosâ-
wamah, sharyah

Barrel, برميل barmeel

Barley, شعير shaعir

Basket, زنبيل zanbeel

Beard, لحية li'hyah

Beautiful, جميل jameel

Before, قبل * اوّل ćabl, awwal

Begin, v. ابتدا ibtada

Beginning, ابتدآ * بدء ibtida,
badء

Believe, v. صدّق sadda'k

Beyond, ورآء warâ

Big, ضخم 'daćhm

Bird, طير 'tyre

Bite, عضّ عa'dd

Bitter, مرّ morr

Blame, v. وبّخ * لام lâm,
wabbaćh

Bleed, أدَمَي adma

Blessing, بركة baracah

Blossom (flower), نَوّر nour;
كمّ cimm

Blow, ضربة 'darbah

Body, جسد * جسم jism, jasad

Bold, جسور jasoor

Bolt, ضبّ 'dabb

Book, كتاب kitâb

Bookseller, بائع الكتب bâiع
al cotob

Borrow, استعار istaعâr

Bottle, قنّينة 'kinnînah

Bottom, قعر 'kaعr

Bough, فرع farع

Bought, مشتري moshtara

Bow, قوس 'house

Box, صندوق 'sandoo'k

Branch, غصن * فرع go'sn, farع

Brass, نحاس na'hâs

Brave, جريٴ jarie

Bread, عيش * خبز ćhobz,
عishe

Breadth, عَرْض عar'd

Break, v. كسر casar

Breath, نفس nafas

Brick, اجُرّ âjorr

Bride, عروس عaroos

Bridegroom, عروس * عريس
عaroos, عaris

Bridle, لجام lijâm

Bright, بهيّ bahi

Bring, *imp.* هات * احضر a'h-'dir, hât

Brought, أُحْضر o'h'dir

Brush, فرشه forshah

Build, بني bana

Burn, *v. a.* and *v. n.* احترق i'htàra'k

Busy, مشغول mashgool

Buy, *v.* اشتري ishtara

C

Cabbage, كرنب * ملفوف co-ronb, malfoof

Cable, حبل 'habl

Cage, قفص ćafa's

Cake, كعك k¿ak

Calf, عجل ¿ijl

Calm (of the sea), ساكن sâkin

Camel, جمل jamal

Camp, معسكر mo¿ascar

Candle, شمع sham¿

Captain, قبطان 'kaptân

Care, اهتمام * عناية ¿inâyah, ihtimâm

Careful, حريص * مهتم 'harîs, mohtamm

Carpenter, نجّار najjâr

Carpet, سجّاده sajjâdah

Carry, حمل 'hamal

Cash, نقد na'kd

Cask, برميل barmîl

Catch, *s.* قبض * أَخْذ ac'hth, ćab'd

Cause, سبب sabab

Cautious, محترز mo'htariz

Celebrated, مشهور mashhoor

Certain, محقق mo'ha'kka'k

Chain, *s.* سلسله salsalah

Chair, كرسي corsi

Change, *v.* بدّل baddal

Charge (to order), وصي wa'ssa

Cheap, رخيص ra'chî's

Cheat, *v.* غش gashsh

Chicken, فروج farrooj

Child, ولد walad

Choose, *v.* اختار ićhtâr

Circle, دائرة dâirah

Circumstance, حال 'hâl

City, مدينة madînah

Civil (polite), متأدّب mo-taaddib

Clean, نظيف nazîf

Clever, حاذق شاطر shâ'tir, 'hâthi'k

Climb, ارتقآ irtiĉâ

Clock, ساعة sâ̧ah

Clothe, v. البس * كسا casa, albas

Cloud سحاب sa'hâb

Coach, عربايه * كروسه carroo-sah, ̧arabayah

Coast, ساحل sâ'hil

Cold, برد bard

Colour, لون loune

Comb, مشط mosh't

Come, imp. تعال ta̧âla

Comfort, راحة * هنآ ra'hah, hanâ

Commence, ابتدا ibtada

Commerce, متجر matjar

Common, مشترك * دون mosh-tarak, doon

Communicate (inform), v. اعلم a̧alam

Companion, رفيق rafi'k

Company, s. جمعية jam̧iyah

Compare, v. قايس ĉâyas

Compass, بيكار bicâr

Compassion, شفقة shafa'kah

Compel, v. الزم * احوج alzam, a'hwaj

Competent, قادر * جدير ĉâdir, jadîr

Complain, تشكّي tashakka

Complete, تكميل takmeel

Comply, (consent), v. قبل * 'cabil, رضي ra'di

Comprehend, فهم fahim

Conceal, v. a. كتم * اخفي aéh-fa, catam

Conclude (finish), ختم ĉha-tam

Conclusion, ختام ĉhitâm

Condemn, حكم بالموت 'hacam bil mout

Condition, حال * شرط shar't, 'hâl

Conduct (on the road), v. شيّع * وصّل shy-ya̧, wa'ssal

Confess, اقرار i´krâr

Confidence, ايتمان*ثقه thi´kah, itimân

Conquer, غلب * قهر ´kahar, galab

Conquered, مغلوب magloob

Consent, v. رضي ra´di

Consent, s. رضي rida

Consequence (in), نتچة nati-jah

Consider, تامّل * اعتبر i´eta-bar, ta-ammal

Consult, شاور shâwar

Contain, v. اشتمل ishtamal

Contented, قانع * راضي râ´di, ´kâniع

Continue, v. استمّر istamarr

Contrary, خلاف châlâf

Contrive, ارتأي irta-â

Convenient, مناسب * ملائم monâsib, molâim

Conversation, مخاطبة moĉhâ-´tabah

Convey, نقل naĉal

Cook, طباخ ´tabbâĉh

Cool, رطب ra´tb

Cord, حبل ´habl

Cork, سدادة sidâdah

Corn, قطاني * قمح ´kam´h, ´ka-´tâni

Cost, ثمن thaman

Cotton, قطن ĉo´tn

Cough, سعال soعâl

Count, v. حسب * عدّ عadd, ´hasab

Country, بلاد * ريف bilâd, reef

Courage, جرآة jarâ-ah

Credit (at), دين dine

Crooked, اعوج عwaj

Crowd, زحام zi´hâm

Cry, v. صرخ ´saraĉh

Cultivate, v. (the ground) حرث ´harath

Cunning, مكّار makkâr

Cup, فنجان * قدح ´kada´h, finjân

Cure, داوي dâwa

Curious, عجيب عajib

Curtain, ستاره sitârah

D

Damp, رطب * ندي ra´tb, nadi

Dance, v. رقص raćas

Dare, v. تجاسر tajâsar

Darkness, ظلام zalâm

Daughter, بنت bint

Day, نهار nahâr

Dear (not cheap), غزال gazâl

Debt, دين dine

Deceive, v. خدع ćhadaع

Decide, جزم jazam

Deep, عميق aمî´k

Delay, تأخير tâćhîr

Delightful, مفرح * سارّ sârr, mofarri´h

Delighted, مسرور masroor

Deliver, تسليم taslim

Demand, v. طلب ´talab

Deny, v. انكار incâr

Depend, توقف علي * تعلّق ب taعalla´k, tawa´k´kaf

Deprive, حرم من ´haram

Description, وصف wa´saf

Deserve, مستحقّ mosta´hi´k´k

Desire, رغبة ragbah

Desirous, راغب râgib

Despair, يئس ya-is

Despise, v. احتقر i´htaćar

Destroy, دمّر * اهلك dammar, ahlak

Detain, امسك * حبس * عوّق عou-wa´k, ´habas, amsak

Determine, v. جزم jazam

Diamond, الماس * ماس mâs, almâs

Difference, فرق * خلاف far´k, ćhilâf

Different, مخالف moćhâlif

Difficult, صعب ´saعb

Difficulty, صعوبة ´soعoubah

Dig, حفر ´hafar

Diligent, s. مجتهد mojtahid

Dine, z. تغدّي tagadda

Dinner, غدآ gadâ

Dirty, وسخ wasićh

Disagreeable, مكروه makrooh

Discontented, غير راضي gire râ´di

Discourse, حديث * خطاب ´chi´tâb, ´hadîth

Discretion, رشد * تمييز tam-yeez, roshd

Dishes, صحاف * صحون 'so'hoon, 'sihâf

Dishonest, غير امين gire amîn

Dislike, s. كره carih

Dismiss, v. عزل * صرف 'saraf, azal

Disobey, عصي a'sa

Displease, اغتاظ igtâz

Dispose (of), تصرّف في ta's-'sarf fi

Dispute, v. جادل jâdal

Distance, بعد bo ed

Distinguish, ميّز my-yaz

Distress, كرب carb

Do, v. فعل fa eal

Doctor, طبيب 'tabîb

Doubtful, مريب * ملتبس morîb, moltabis

Draw, v. جرّ * سحب jarr, sa'hab

Dress, v. a. البس * كسا casa, albas

Dressing, ملبس molbis

Drive (out of a country), v. طرد 'tarad

Drink, v. شرب sharib

Drop, s. نقطة no'ktah

Drum, طبل 'table

Dry, ناشف nâshif

Duck, بطّة ba'ttah

Duty, فرض * واجب far'd, wâjib

Dwell, سكن sacan

E.

Ear, اذن othn, ozn

Earn, v. كسب casab

Earnest, جدّ jidd

Earth, أرض ar'd

Earthenware, فخّار fac'hc'hâr

Easy, سهل sahl

Eat, v. اكل acal

Edge (of a sword), حدّ 'hadd

Education, تربية tarbiyah

Effect (trace), اثر athar

Egg, بيضه by'dah

Elegant. ظريف zarîf

Eloquence, فصاحة fa'sâ'hah

Empire, سلطنة sal'tanah

Employ (make use of), v. استعمل istaɛmal

Employment, استخدام istic'h-dâm

Empty, فارغ fârigh

Encourage, v. رغّب * شجّع shajjaɛ, raggab

Endeavour, v. اجتهد * حاول 'hâwal, ijtahad

Enemy, عدو ɛadoo

Engagement, ارتباط irtibâ't

England, انكلترة Ínkilterrah

Entirely, بالكلّية bil colliyah

Equal, مساوي mosâwi

Error, غلط gala't

Escape, v. نجا * افلت naja, aflat

Establish, انشا * ثبت thabbat, ansha

Estate, املاك * عقار amlâk, ɛa'câr

Eternal, ابديّ abadee

Even (as), حقّي * بل bal, 'hatta

Evening, مسآ masâ

Event, واقعه wâ-'kiɛah

Evidence, شهادة shahâdah

Evil, شرّ * سو soo, sharr

Europe, اوربا ourobba

Exact, محرّر * مضبوط ma'd-boo't, mo'harrar

Example, عبرة * مثال mithâl, ɛibrah

Excellent, فاضل * بارع fâ'dil, bâriɛ

Excuse, عذر ɛothr

Execute (to kill), قتل 'ka-tal

Expect, انتظر intazar

Expense, مصروف ma'sroof

Experience, اختبار * تجربة ic'h-tibâr, tajribah

Explain, شرح shara'h

Explanation, تفسير tafsir

Express (messenger), ساعي sâɛi

Extensive, مديد madîd

Extent, امتداد imtidâd

Extraordinary, خلاف العاده c'hilâf alɛâdah

F.

Extravagant, مسرف *mosrif*

Eye, عين *eine*

Fable, خرافة * مثل *chorâfah, mathal*

Face, وجه *wajh*

Fag (tire), v. اعيا *aeya*

Fail (bankrupt), افلس *aflas*

Faint, v. وَنَي * ضعف *wana, 'daeof*

Fair (weather), لطيف *la'tîf*

Faithful, امين *amîn*

Fall, v. وقوع *wo'kooe*

False, زور *zoor*

Family, عيلة *eylah*

Famine, قحط *'ka'ht*

Fancy, خيال * وَهْم *chayâl, wahm*

Fat, سمين *samîn*

Father, اب *ab*

Fatigue, تعب *taeab*

Fault, عيب * نقيصه *eibe, na'kisah*

Faultless, بلا عيب *bila eibe*

Favour, منة * نعمة *minnah, niemah*

Favourable, مستحب مرضي *mar'di, most'habb*

Favourite, مستحب * مفضّل *mofa'd'dal, mostahabb*

Fear, v. خوف *c'houf*

Fearful, s. مخوف *خائف *châîf, machoof*

Feast, عيد *ead*

Feather, ريش *reash*

Features, ملامح *اسارير *asârir, malâmi'h*

Feed, v. اطعم * مان * علف *ealaf, mân, a't eam*

Fed, معلوف *maeloof*

Feel, حسّ *'hiss*

Female, انثي *ontha*

Ferry, معبر *maebar*

Fetch, جاب *jâb*

Few, قليل *'kalîl*

Field, حقل *'ha'kl*

Fight, v. and s. قتال *'kitâl*

Find, v. وجد *wajad*

Finish, v. اتمّ *atamm*

Fish, سمك * حوت samak, 'hoot

Fisherman, صيّاد sy-yâd

Fix, v. قرر * انبت athbat, 'karrar

Flag, عَلَم alam

Fling (to throw), رمى rama

Flint, صوان 'saw-wan

Floor, حضيض 'ha'di'd

Flour, دقيق * طحين 'ta'hîn, da'ki'k

Flower, زهره zahrah

Fly, v. طار 'târ

Fly, v. (runaway), هرب harab

Food, قوت * طعام 'koot, 'ta-âm

Foolish, احق a'hma'k

Forbid, منع * نهي naha, ma-na

Force, قوة 'koowah

Forehead, جبين jabin

Foreign, غريب * اجني garîb, ajnabi

Forest, غابة gâbah

Forget, v. نسي nasi

Forgive, غفر gafar

Former (the), سابق * مقدم sâbi'k, mo'kaddam

Formidable (to be feared) مهول * مهيب mahîb, mahool

Forsake, هجر * ترك tarak, ha-jar

Fortune, قسمة * بخت ba'ht, 'kismah

Foundation, اساس asâs

Fountain, عين * ينبوع ine, yanboo

Fowl, طير 'tire

Freedom (one's own will), اختيار ichtiyâr

Friend, حبيب 'habîb

Friendly, بمحبة bima'habbah

Frequent, انتاب * تردد علي taraddad, intâb

Fresh, جديد * طري 'tari, jadîd

Fruit, فاكهة fâkihah

Full, متلي momtali

Furnish, جهز jahhaz

Furniture (of a house) فرش * جهاز farsh, jihâz

Future, آتي * مستقبل *âti, mos-
      ta′kbil

G.

Gain, كسب kasab

Garden, بستان bostân

Gather, جمع jamaε

General (of brigade), جنرال
      general

Generally, عموماً * غالباً εomoo-
      man, gâliban

Generosity, سخا * كرم caram,
      saćha

Gentle, لطيف la′tîf

Gentleman, خواجه c′hawâja

Geography, جغرافيه jagrâfia

Girl, بنت bint

Give, v. اعطي aε′ta

Glad, فرحان far′hân

Glass, زجاج zojâj

Gloves, كفوف cofoof

Go, v. راح * ذهب thahab,
      râ′h

Gold, ذهب thahab

Good, طيّب 'ty-ib

Govern, v. حكم 'hacam

Government, حكومة 'hocoo-
      mah

Grand, عظيم εazim

Grandeur, عظمة εazamah

Grant, v. انعم anεam

Grapes, عنب εinab

Grass, عشب oshb

Grateful, شكور shacoor

Gratitude, شكران النعمة sho-
      crân anniεmah

Great, عظيم εazim

Green, اخضر aćh′dar

Ground, s. ارض ar′d

Grow, نمي nama

Guide, s. دلالة dalâlah

Guide, v. دليل daleel

H.

Habit, عادة εâdah

Hair, شعر shaεr

Half, نصف ni′sf

Hand, يد yad

Handkerchief, منديل mandeel

Handsome, جميل jameel

Happened (it), اتفق * جري
   jara, ittafa'k

Happiness, غبطة * سعادة *gib-*
   *'tah, sa*ع*adah*

Happy, سعيد *sa*ع*ead*

Hard, قاسي * يابس *yâbis, 'kâsi*

Hardship, قساوة *'kasâwah*

Haste, عجلة ع*ajalah*

Hasten, استعجل *ista*ع*jal*

Harmless, بلاضرر *bila 'darar*

Hat, برنيطه *borny'tah*

Hate, v. ابغض *abga'd*

Have v. حصل علي *ha'sal* ع*ala*

Hay, برسيم *barsim*

Head, راس *râs*

Hear, v. سمع *sami*ع

Heart, قلب *'kalb*

Heavy, ثقيل *tha'keel*

Heal (cure), v. شفي *shafa*

Help, v. ساعد *sâ*ع*ad*

Help, s. مساعدة *mosâ*ع*adah*

Hill, تلّ *tall*

Hindrance, منع * تعويق *man*ع*,
   ta*ع*wee'k*

Hire, v. a. اكري *akra*

History, تاريخ *târeec'h*

Hold, v. مسك *masak*

Hole, s. خرق *c'har'k*

Home, وطن *wa'tan*

Honey, عسل ع*asal*

Honour, عرض * شرف ع*ir'd,
   sharaf*

Hope, امل *amal*

Horn, قرن *'karn*

Hot, سخن *sóchn*

Holy, طاهر *'tâhir*

Hour, ساعة *sâ*ع*ah*

House, بيت * دار *dâr, bite*

Humanity, انسانية *insâniyah*

Hunger, جوع *joo*ع

Hungry, v. جوعان *jou*ع*ân*

Hurt, v. آذي *âtha*

Husband, زوج * بعل *zouj, ba*ع*l*

I.

Idea, فكر *fikr*

Idle, كسلان *caslân*

Ignorance, جهل *jahl*

Ignorant, جاهل *jâhil*

K

Ill, مريض mari'd

Illness, مرض mara'd

Imagine, تصوّر ta'saw-or

Immediate, حالي 'hâlee

Immense, وافر wâfir

Imperfect, ناقص nâ'ki's

Important (affair), مهمّ mo-himm

Impossible, غيرممكن * محال mo'hâl, gire momkin

Improbable, غير محمّل gire mo'htamil

Improper, غيرمناسب gire mo-nâsib

Imprudence, تهوّر tahawor

Improve (to), جود * حسّن 'hassan, jawwad

Impropriety, عدم مناسبة eadam monâsabah

Impure, غيرخالص gire c'hali's

Incapable, غيرقادر gire 'kâdir

Incessant, متواصل * دائم dâ-im, motawâ-'sil

Inclination, ميل mile

Inclined, مائل mâ-il

Include (a letter), ضـمّـن 'damman

Income, دخل * ايراد irâd, dac'hl

Incomplete, غيرتامّ giretâmm

Inconvenient, غير موافق gire mowâfi'k

Incorrect, غيرصحيح gire 'sa-'hi'h

Increase, زيادة ziyâdah

Indifferent, بغير فرق bigiri far'k

Indisposition, انحراف مـزاج in'hirâf mizâj

Infancy, طفولية 'tofooli-yah

Infant, طفل 'tifl

Inferior, ادني * دون doon, adna

Infinite, غيرمتناهي gire mo-tanâhi

Influence, تاثير * نفوذ nofooth, tatheer

Inform, اخبار ic'hbâr

Information, خبر c'habar

Ingenious, المعّي almaعi

Inhabitant, ساكن sâhin

Inhuman, عدم انسانية adam insâniyah

Injure, v. ضرّ darr

Injury, ضرر darar

Innocence, برآءة barâ-ah

Innocent, بري bari

Insecure, غير مضمون gire ma'dmoon

Insensibility, عته * جنون jo-noon

Insincere, غير مخلص gire moc'hli's

Insolent, سفيه safih

Instant (ready), حاضر hâ'dir

Instruct, درّب * عرّف * علّم allam, arraf, darrab

Insufficient, غير كافي gire câfi

Intelligent, فهيم fahim

Intention, نيّة ni-yah

Interest (advantage), فائدة fâ-idah

Interfere, v. يتداخل yata-dâc'hal

Interpret, v. ترجم tarjam

Interpreter, ترجان tarjomân

Interrupt, قطع 'katae

Invent, اخترع ic'htarae

Investigation, بحث ba'hth

Invincible, غير مغلوب gire magloob

Invite, دعا daae

Irregular, غير مرتّب gire mo-rattab

Island, جزيرة jazeerah

J.

Jar, جرّة jarrah

Jealous, غيور ga-yoor

Jest, مزح maz'h

Jewel, جوهر jouhar

Join, v. وصل wa'sal

Journal, جرنال jornâl

Journey, سفر safar

Joy, فرح fara'h

Joyful, فرحان far'hân

Judge, v. حكم * قضي 'hacam, 'ca'da

Judgment, حكم * قضا 'hokm, ca'dâ

Juice (lemon), عصير a'seer

Jump, قفز * وثب ʼkafaz, wa-
thab

Just, محق * عادل moʼhiʼkʼk,
ɛâdil

Justice, حق * عدل ʼhaʼkʼk,
ɛadl

K.

Keel, قعر المركب ʼkaɛr al-
marcab

Keen (sharp), حادّ ʼhâdd

Keep, v. حفظ * ابقي ʼhafiz,
abʼka

Kept, محفوظ maʼhfooz

Kettle, غلّايه galla-yah

Key, مفتاح miftâʼh

Kill, v. قتل ʼcatal

Kind (sort), نوع nouɛ

Kindness, احسان * رفق ʼrifʼk,
iʼhsân

King, ملك malik

Kingdom, مملكة mamlacah

Kiss, v. باس * قبّل bâs, ʼcab-
bal

Knee, ركبة rokbah

Kneel, ركع * جثا racaɛ,
jatha

Knife, سكين sikkeen,

Knock, v. قرع ʼkaraɛ

Know, عرف ɛaraf

Knowledge, معرفة maɛrifah

L.

Laborious, كادّ * مجدّ mo-jidd,
câdd

Labour, كدّ cadd

Labourer, كادّ câdd

Lady, ست sitt

Lake, بحيرة boʼhyrah

Lame, اعرج aɛraj

Lament, ناح nâʼh

Lamp, مسرجة masrajah

Land, عقار * ارض arʼd, ɛaɛâr

Language, لسان * لغة lisân,
logah

Large, كبير * واسع wâsiɛ, cabeer

Last, آخر âchir

Laugh, v. ضحك ʼdaʼhik

Lawful, حلال * شرعي sharɛi,
ʼhalâl

Lay up (store), اذخر *iththa char*

Lazy, كسلان *caslân*

Lead, رصاص *ra'sâ's*

Leaf, ورقة *waracáh*

Lean, adj. مهزول * نحيف *mahzool, na'hîf*

Leap, طفر *'tafar*

Learn, تعلّم *taعallam*

Learned, عالم *عâlim*

Learning, علم *عilm*

Least, اقل *a'call*

Leave, v. أذن *azin, athin*

Left (hand), شمال *shimâl*

Lend, اعار * سـاف *sallaf, aعâr*

Leisure, فراغ *farâg*

Leg, ساق *sâ'k*

Lemon, ليمون *lymoon*

Length, طول *'tool*

Let (a house), اكري *acra*

Liberty, حرّية *'horri-yah*

Lick, v. لحس *la'has*

Lie (to recline), اتّكا *ittaca*

Lie, s. كذب *cathib*

Lie, v. كذب *cathab*

Life, حياة * عمر *عomr, 'ha-yâh*

Light, adj. خفيف *c'haf'if*

Light, s. نور *noor*

Lightning, برق *bar'k*

Like (similar), مثل *mithl*

Lion, اسد *asad*

Liquid, مائع *mâ-iع*

Live, v. عاش *عâsh,*

Load, s. حمّل *'hammal*

Loaf, رغيف *ragîf*

Lock, قفل *'cofl*

Lodge, ماوي *ma-wa*

Long, adj. طويل *'ta-weel*

Looking-glass, مرآة *mirâk, mirayeh*

Loose (to let), خلّي *c'halla*

Lose, فقد * خسر *faعad, c'hasir,*

Lost, مفقود * ضائع *mafعood, 'dâ-iع*

Love, s. محبة * عشق *ma'hab-bah, عish'k*

Low, سافل *sâfil,*

Luggage, اثقال * عفش *عafsh, athعâl*

M.

Machine, آلة *âlah*

Magazine, مخزن *mac'hzin*

Magnificent جليل *jalîl*

Maid, بنت * جارية *bint, jâ-riyah*

Majesty, عظمة *azamah*

Make, v. عمل *amil*

Made, معمول *maɛmool*

Manage, دبّر *dabbar*

Mankind, انسان *insân*

Manner, منوال *minwâl*

Manufactory معمل * كرخانة *carc'hânah, maɛmal*

Map, خرطه *c'har'tah*

Marble, مرمر *marmar*

March, v. مشي * زحف علي *masha, za'haf*

Mare, فرس *faras*

Market, سوق *soo'k*

Marriage, زواج *zawâj*

Marry, تزوج *tazaw-waj*

Master, معلّم *moɛallim*

Mean (sordid), خسيس *c'ha-sees*

Means (occasion), وسيله *wa-silah*

Measure, قياس *'kiyâs*

Meat, لحم * طعام *la'hm, 'taɛâm*

Meet, v. لاقي *lâ'ka*

Melon, بطيخ *bi'ttic'h*

Melt, ذاب *thâb*

Memory, ذكر * ذاكرة *thâkirah, thikr*

Mend, اصلح *a'sla'h*

Merciful, رحوم *ra'hoom*

Merchandise, بضاعة * تجارة *tijârah, bi'dâɛah*

Merchant, تاجر *tâjir*

Mercury, زيبق *ziba'k*

Middle, وسط *wasa't*

Mild, حلم * لطيف *halîm, la'tîf*

Milk, حليب * لبن *laban, 'halîb*

Mill, طاحونة *'ta'hoonah*

Mind, s. بال * عقل *bâl, a'kl*

Mine, لى * متاعي *matâɛ, li*

Mirth, طرب*فرح *fara'h, 'tarab*

Mischief, سوء *soo*

Miserable, شقي *sha'ki*

Misery, شقاوة *s'ha'kâwah*

Mismanagement, سوء تدبير soo tadbeer

Mistake, غلط gala't

Mix, v. خلط * مزج mazaj, c'hala't

Moderate, v. عدّل adddal

Modern, متأخر*محدث mo'h-dath, mota-ac'h c'hir

Modesty, حشمة 'hishmah

Moment, دقيقة da'ki'kah

Moon, قمر 'camar

Mountain, جبل jabal

Mud, وحل wa'hl

Mule, بغل bagl

Mutual, مشترك moshtarak

Myrtle, آس âs

Mystery سرّ sirr

N.

Nail, مسمار * ظُفر zofr, mis-mâr

Naked, عريان oryân

Name, اسم ism

Narrow, ضيّق 'dy-i'k

Nation, امة ommah

Native, بلديّ * متولّد baladi, motawallid

Nature, طبيعة 'tabî؏ah

Natural, طبيعي 'tabî؏

Naughty, قبيح 'kabi'h

Navigation, سفر البحر safar al ba'hr

Near, قريب 'karîb

Neat, ظريف * نظيف nazif, zarif

Necessary, لازم lâzim

Need, احتياج i'hti-yâj

Neglect, v. اهمل ahmal

Negligent, مهمل mohmil

Neighbour, جار jâr

Net, شبكة shabacah

New, جديد jadîd

Next قريب * قابل (day), 'ka-reeb, 'kâbil

Nice, حسن*طيب hasan,'ty-ib

Night, ليل lile

Noise, ضجة 'dajjah

None, لا احد * لا شي lâ a'had, lâ shy

Nonsense, هذيان hathayân

GOAL—J

Nothing, شي لا *là shy*

Notice, s. علم* خبر *ilm, c'ha-bar*

Nourish, غذّي *gaththa*

Novelty, جدّة *jiddah*

Number, عدد *adad*

Numerous, عديد *adîd*

Nurse, s. مرضعه * دايه *mordi-ah dâyah*

O.

Oak, بطم *bo'tm*

Oar, مقداف *mi'kdâf*

Oath, قسم * يمين *yamîn, ća-sam*

Obedience, طاعة *tâ'ah*

Obedient, طائع *tâ-i'*

Obey, اطاع *a'tâ'*

Object, v. اعترض *i'târa'd*

Object, s. شي* حاجه *hâjah, shy*

Objection, اعتراض *i'tirâ'd*

Oblige, v. من علي *mann ala*

Obscure, خامل * غامض *châ-mil, gâmi'd*

Observe, v. لاحظ *lâ'haz*

Obstacle, مانع *mâni'*

Obstinate, عنيد *anid*

Obtain, تحصيل *ta'h'seel*

Occasion, فرصة * داعي *forśah, dâ'i*

Occupy, v. استعمل * شغل *sha-gal, ista'mal*

Occur, v. جري* وقع *jara, waća'*

Occurrence, وقوع *wo'koo'*

Odd (strange), غريب*) num-ber), فرد * بدع *garib, fard, bid'*

Offence, اساءة *isâ-ah*

Offend, v. اساء *asâ*

Offer, قدّم * اعطي *'kaddam, a'ta*

Office, وظيفة *wazîfah*

Officer, ذو وظيفة * ضابط *'dâ-bi't, thoo wazîfah*

Oil, زيت *zite*

Omit, حذف *'hathaf*

Omnipotent (the), قادر علي كل شي *'kâdir ala coll shy*

Opinion, مذهب * ظن *math-hab, zann*

Opportunity, فرصة *forsah*

Opposition, مقابلة *mocâbalah*

Orange, بردقان *bordocân*

Orator, خطيب * هاتف *châ'tîb, hâtif*

Order, s. ترتيب * وصية *tartib, wa-'siyah*

Origin, اصل *âsl*

Ornament, زينة *zinah*

Out, خارج * برّا *c'hârij, barra*

Outside, في الخارج *fi al c'hârij*

Over, فوق *fou'k*

Overcome, غلب *galab*

Overflow, طفح *'tafa'h*

Overset, قلب * ركس *'ka-lab, racas*

Overtake, v. ادرك * لحق *ad-rak, la'hi'k*

Own, خاصّ *c'hâ'ss*

Owner, مالك * صاحب *sâ'hib, mâlik*

P.

Pack, صرة *sorrah*

Pail, دلو *dalwo*

Pain, وجع *waja*

Paint, صوّر *saw-war*

Pale, a. اصفر *asfar*

Parcel, حزمة * صرة *'sorrah, 'hozmah*

Pardon, عفو *afwo*

Parents, الاب والام *al ab wa-lomm*

Parrot, ببغا * درة *dorrah, babbaga*

Partake, اشترك في *ishtarak*

Particular, مخصوص *mach-'soo's*

Party, جاعة *jamâ'ah*

Pass, v. مرّ * عبر *abar, marr*

Passage (of troops), مرور *mo-roor*

Passenger, مسافر * مار *mârr, mosâfir*

Passport, جواز * تذكرة السفر *tathkirat assafar, jawâz*

Passion (anger), غضب *ga-'dab*

Passionate, غضوب *ga'doob*

Paste, طلاۤ *'tilâ*

Path, مسلك * ممر mamarr,
maslak

Patience, صبر 'sabr

Patient, صبور 'saboor

Pause, v. وقف waćaf

Pay, في * ادّي wafa, adda

Payment, ادآ * وفآ wafâ, adâ

Peace, سلام * صلح salâm,
'sol'h

Penalty, نكال * غرامة grâmah,
naćâl

Pen, قلم ćalam

Penknife مبراة القلم mibrât
alćalam

Pepper, فلفل folfol

Perceive, شعر * دري shaعar,
dara

Perfect, كامل câmil

Perfection, كمال camâl

Perform, عمل عamil

Perfume, v. بخر * عطر عa'ttar,
bac'hćhar

Permission, اجازة ijâzah

Permit, اجاز * سمح ajâz, sa-
ma'h

Perplexed, حيران 'hyrân

Persevere, واظب wâzab

Perseverance, مواظبة mowá-
zabah

Persuade, اقنع a'knaع

Petition, عرض حال عar'd 'hâl

Phial (small bottle), حنجور
'honjoor

Phrase, جلة * عبارة jomlah,
عibârah

Physic, دوآ dawâ

Physician, مداوي * طبيب 'tabîb, modâwi

Pickles, مخلّل moćhallal

Picture, صورة 'soorah

Piece, قطعة 'ki'tعah

Pig, خنزير ćhinzeer

Pillar, عمود عamood

Pincers, ملقط mil'ka't

Pious, تقي ta'ki

Pit, حفرة 'hofrah

Pity, شفقة shafa'kah

Place, موضع mou'diع

Plague, وبآ * طاعون tâعoon,
wabâ

Plain, s. بسيط * صريح basî't, 'sarî'h

Plank, لوح lou'h

Plate, صحن * صحفة 'sa'hn, 'sa'hfah

Play, v. لعب laعib

Pleasant, سارّ * مرضي mar'di, sârr

Pleasure, حظ * لذة laththah, 'hazz

Please, ارضي * اعجب aعjab, ar'da

Plenty, وفور * كثرة cathrah, wofoor

Plough, حرث 'harath

Poet, شاعر shâعir

Poetry, شعر shiعr

Point (of a knife or needle), راس * حدّ 'hadd, râs

Politeness, ادب * كياسة adab, kiyâsah

Pony, مهر mohr

Poor, فقير fa'keer

Possess, ملك malak

Possible, ممكن momkin

Poverty, فقر fa'kr

Power, قدرة 'kodrah

Powerful, قادر kâdir

Practice, عادة * ممارسة عâdah, momârasah

Praise, v. مدح * جد 'hamid, mada'h

Prayer, صلوة * دعا 'salâh, doعâ

Prefer, فضـل * رجّح raj-ja'h, fa'ddal

Prejudice, ضرر 'darar

Prepare, اعدّ aعadd

Presence, حضـور 'ho'door

Present, s. هدية hadi-yah

Preserve, v. حفظ * صان 'hafiz, 'sân

Pretence, دعوي * تعلل daعwa, taعallol

Pretty, كويس cowyyes

Prevail, v. غلب galab

Prevent, منع manaع

Pride, كبر kibr

Print, v. طبع 'tabaع

Prisoner, اسير asîr

Private (in), خلوة c'halwah

Probable, محمل *mo'htamil*

Proceed, تقدم *istamarr, ta'kaddam*

Procure, v. حصل * استظهر به *'ha'ssal*

Produce, v. انتج اغل * *antaj, agall*

Produce, s. غلة *gallah*

Promise, s. وعد *waعd*

Pronounce, لفظ *lafaz*

Proof, دليل *dalîl*

Proper, مناسب *monâsib*

Prosperous, موفق * ناجح *mowaffa'k, nâji h*

Protect, حمي *اجار* *'hama, ajâr*

Proud, متكبر *motacabbir*

Providence, عناية الله *inâyat Allah*

Province, ايالة *iyâlah*

Provisions, ذخيرة *thaćhîrah*

Prudence, حزم * بصيرة *'hazm, ba'sîrah*

Pull, v. جذب *jathab*

Pulse, نبض *nab'd*

Punishment, عذابعathâb

Purchase, v. اشتري *ishtara*

Pure, خالص * نقي *na'hi,ćhâli's*

Purpose, قصد *'ka'sd*

Purse, كيس *kees*

Pursue, v. طارد *'târad*

Put, وضعع *wa'da*

Q.

Quail (a bird), سمان *sommân*

Qualifications, صفة *'sifah*

Quality (good qualities) كيفية *kyfi-yah*

Quantity, مقدار * كمية *mi'k-dâr, cammiyah*

Quarrel, v. نازعع *nâza*

Queen, ملكة *malikah*

Quench, اطفا *a'tfa*

Quick, سريعع *sarî*

Quince, سفرجل *safarjal*

Quill, ريش *reesh*

Quit, ترك *tarak*

Quiet, ساكن * مطمئن *mo't-ma-inn, sâkin*

Quote, v. نقل * اورد *naćal, owrad*

Quotation, نقل * ايراد na'kl, irâd.

R.

Rabbit, ارنب arnab

Rags, رعابيل raẹâbil

Rain, s. مطر ma'tar

Rain, v. مطر ma'tar

Raisins, زبيب zabîb

Rank (soldiers), صف 'saff

Rare, نادر nâdir

Rash, متهور motahaw-wir

Raw, في nye

Reach, بلغ balag

Read, قرا 'kara

Real, حقيقي 'ha'kî'ki

Reason, عقل * (cause), سبب a'kl, sabab

Receive, تسلّم tasallam

Receipt, s. سند * رجعة sanạd, rajẹah

Recent, حادث * حديث 'hâ-dith, 'hadîth

Reckon, حسب hasab

Recollect, تذكّر tathakkar

Recommend, نوّه به * وصّي wa'ssa, now-wah

Recompense, مجازاه * مكافاه mocâfâh, mojâzâh

Recover, استردّ * افاق ista-radd, afâ'k

Recovery (of health), افاقة ifâ'kah

Reflect, فكّر fakkar

Refresh, اراح * طرّي 'tarra, arâ'h

Refusal, اباآ ibâ

Refuse, ابي aba

Regiment, الاي alaï

Regret, v. تاسّف ta-assaf

Regular, مرتّب morattab

Rejoice, فرح fari'h

Renew, جدّد jaddad

Rent (of a house), كرا kirâ

Repair (set in order), صلّح * رمم 'salla'h, rammam

Repeat, كرّر carrar

Repentance, ندامة nadâ-mah

Reply, جاوب jâwab

Report, اشاع * قرّر carrar, ashâ ع

Reproach, v. لام * وبّخ lâm, wabbaćh

Request, v. طلب * التمس ta-lab, iltamas

Reside, مكث macath

Resist, مانع * قاوم câwam, mâna ع

Resolute, ذو عزيمة thoo azî-mah

Resolve, v. عزم azam

Rest, v. استراح istarâ'h

Rest, s. استراحة * راحة râ'hah

Restless, بلاراحة bila râ'hah

Result, حاصل * نتيجة natîjah, 'hâ'sil

Retire, انصرف in'saraf

Return, v. رجع raja ع

Revive, احيي a'hya

Reward, جزآ jazâ

Rich, غني ganí

Rice, رز rozz

Ride, v. ركب rakib

Ring, s. خاتم châtim

Rise, v. قام kâm

Robber, لصّ li'ss

Roof, سطح 'sa't'h

Rock, صخر 'sac'hr

Room, بيت * اوضه bite, ou'dah

Root, اصل a'sl

Rope, حبل 'habl

Ruin, خراب c'harâb

Run, جري jara

S.

Sack, زكيبة zakeebah

Sad, كئيب ca-eab

Saddle, سرج sarj

Safe (and sound), مامون * سليم mamoon, salîm

Sail, شراع shirâ ع

Sailor, بحري ba'hri

Salary, جمكية jamki-yah

Sale, بيع beye ع

Sand, رمل raml

Satisfy, v. اكتفي * شبع shabi ع, iktafa

Save, v. خلص c'halla's

Saw, s. منشار minshâr

Scarce, نادر *nâdir*

Sea, بحر *ba'hr*

Search, v. فتش *fattash*

Season, اوان *awân*

Secret, سرّ *sirr*

See, v. نظر *nazar*

Sell, باع *bâ*

Seek, طلب *'talab*

Seed, بزر *bazr*

Seem, ظهر *zahar*

Seize, قبض *kaba'd*

Send, بعث *ba*ath*

Sensible, حساس * عاقل *âkil, 'hassâs*

Sense, (understanding) عقل * (meaning) معي *a'kl, ma*na*

Separate, منفصل * مفرد *mofrad, monfa'sil*

Serious, رزين * جدّ *jidd, razin*

Servant, خدّام *ćhaddâm*

Service, خدمة *'chidmah*

Set (of things), نسق * طقم *nasa'k 'ta'km*

Settle (an affair), اقرّ * انهي *a'ćarr, anha*

Shade, ظلّ *zill*

Shake (a cloth), نفض *nafa'd*

Shame, عيب *chizi, *ibe*

Sharp (knife), حادّ * ذرب *hâdd, tharib*

Shave, v. حلق *'hala'k*

Shelter (-ed place), ملطا * ملجا *malja*

Shine, اشرق * لمع *lama*, ashra'k*

Shoot, رمي *rama*

Shop, حانوت * دكان *'hânoot, doccân*

Short, قصير *'kasîr*

Show, اري * ابدي *abda, ara*

Shut, v. اغلق * سدّ *agla'k, sadd*

Sick, مريض *marîd*

Signal, اشاره * علامه *alâmah, ishârah*

Silence, سكوت *socoot*

Silk, حرير *'harîr*

Sincerity, اخلاص *i'chlâś*

Sin, v. خطيه *c'hatiyah*

Sing, غنّي *ganna*

Sink, v. غرق gari´k

Sit, v. جلس * قعد ćaعad, jalas

Size, جرم jirm

Sky, جوّ * رقيع jow, ra´kiع

Sleep, s. نوم noum

Sleep, v. نام nâm

Small, صغير ´sageer

Smell, شم shamm

Smile, تبسم tabassom

Smoke (of a pipe), v. دخن da´ch´chân

Smooth, ناعم nâعim

Soap, صابون ´saboon

Sober, عفيف عafîf

Society, جعية jamعi-yah

Soft, ناعم * ليّن nâعim, ly-ien

Solid, متين matîn

Something, بعض شي baعd shy

Sorrow, حزن ´hozn

Sort, شكل * نوع nouع, shakl

Soul, نفس nafs

Sound, adj. صحيح sa´hi´h

Sour, حامض ´hâmi´d

Space, مدي mada

Spare, v. ابقى علي ab´ka عala

Speak, v. تكلم tacallam

Spectacles, نظّارات nazzârât

Spend, صرف ´saraf

Spice, بهار bahâr

Split, v. شقّ * صدع sha´k´k, sadaع

Spoiled, متلف * مخسّر moc´has-sar, motlaf

Spot, موضع * شين shine, mou´diع

Spread, v. بسط basa´t

Spring, (of water) عين * ينبوع yanbouع, عine

Sprinkle, رش rashsh

Stairs, درج daraj

Stand, v. قام ´kâm

Starving, تفقّر ta´daw-war

Stay, v. مكث macath

Steady, ثابت * ساكن sâkin, thâbit

Steal, v. سرق sara´k

Steer, تسيير المركب tasyeer al-marcab

Stick, s. عصا ɛaśa

Stiff, يابس yâbis

Still (yet), ايضا ey'dan

Stir, هيج * حرّك 'harrak, hy-yaj

Store, مخزن mac'hzin

Stranger, غريب garîb

Straw, تبن tibn

Strength, قوة 'koowah

Stretch, مدّ madd

Strike, ضرب 'darab

String, s. مرس * خيط 'hi'te, maras

Strip (one's clothes), جرّد jarrad

Strong, قوي 'kawi

Study, درس daras

Subdue, اخضع aćh'daɛ

Submit, اذعن * سلّم a'thɛan, sallam

Succeed, نجح naja'h

Success, نجاح najâ'h

Suck, مصّ ma'ss

Suffer, كابد câbad

Sugar, سكر soccar

Supply, v. امدّ * مار amadd, mâr

Support, v. اسند * اغاث as-nad, agâth

Suppose, v. قدّر * فرض 'kad-dar, fara'd

Supreme, عالي * سامي sâmi, ɛâli

Sure, محقق mo'ha'k'ka'k

Surface, وجه wajh

Surprise, حيّر 'hy-yar

Suspicion, ريب * شبهة ribe, shobhah

Swear, v. اقسم * حالف a'ksam, 'halaf

Sweep, كنس canas

Sweet, حلو 'holow

Swell, v. ورم * انتفخ intafaćh, warim

Swim, سبح * عام saba'h, ɛâm

System, طريقة * قاعدة 'tarî-ćah, ćâɛidah

T.

Take, اخذ aćhath

L

Taken, ماخوذ *mac'hooth*

Talk, تحدث *ta'haddath*

Teach, v. علّم *allam*

Tear, v. (rend) خزّق * مزّق *'chazza'k, mazza'k*

Tell, خبّر *chabbar*

Thank, شكر *shacar*

Thick, تخين *thac'hin*

Think, فكر *faccar*

Thought, فكر *ficr*

Threat, v. تهدد *tahaddad*

Throne, عرش *arsh*

Throw, طرح *'tara'h*

Thunder, رعد *raعd*

Tie, v. ربط *raba't*

Tidings, خبر *'chabar*

Timber, خشب *'chashab*

Time, وقت *wa'kt*

Timid, عاني * هيوب *âni, hayoub*

Tired, ملول *malool*

Tobacco, تبغ * دخان *do'chân, tabg*

Tooth, سن *sinn*

Torch, مشعل *mishعal*

Toss, زجّ *zajj*

Touch, لمس *lamas*

Toy, داح *dâ'h*

Trade, حرفة *'hirfah*

Translation, ترجمة *tarja-mah*

Travel, v. سافر *sâfar*

Tread, وطي *wa'ti*

Treacherous, خائن *'châ-in*

Trifling, زهيد *zahîd*

True, حق *'ha'k'k*

Trust, v. اتكل * ترجّي *tarajja, ittacal*

Truth, حقيقة * حق *'ha'ki'kah*

Try, جرّب *jarrab*

Turn, v.a. ادار *adâr*

Turnip, لفت *lift*

U.

Ugly, قبيح * بشع *bashiع, 'kabî'h*

Umbrella, شمسية * ظُلة *sham-si-yah, zollah*

Unable, v. عاجز *عâjiz*

Unanimous, بلاأسم *bila ism*

Uncertain, غير محقق gire moha'kka'k

Understanding, فهم fahm

Unhappy, شقي sha'ki

Unjust, جائر jâ-ir

Unlocked, غير مقفول gire ma'kfool

Unworthy, غير جدير gire jadîr

Upright, مستقيم mosta'keem

Urgent, مضطر mo'd'tarr

Use, v. استعمل istaᵉmal

Use, s. استعمال * عادة isti-mâl, عâdah

Useful, نافع * مفيد nâfiᵉ, mofîd

Useless, غير نافع gire nâfiᵉ

Utterly, بالكلية bil colli-yah

V.

Vacant, خالي 'châli

Vain, مزهو * باطل bâ'til, mazhoo

Value, قيمة 'kîmah

Valuable, ثمين * نفيس na-fis, thamîn

Various, متنوع motanou wiᵉ

Vanish, أضمحل i'dma'hall

Venture, تجاسر tajâsar

Vexation, تكدير takdeer

Vice, رذيلة ratheelah

Vigilant, منتبه montabih

Violent, عنيف ᵉaneef

Virtue, فضيلة fa'deelah

Visit, زيارة ziyârah

Voice, صوت ṡout

Volume, مجلّد mojallad

Voyage, سفر البحر safar al-ba'hr

W.

Wages, اجرة ojrah

Waggon, عجلة ᵉajalah

Wait, انتظر intazar

Wake, v. a. ايقظ eyᵉaz

Walk, v. مشي masha

Wall, سور * حائط 'hâ-i't, soor

Want, v. احتاج i'htâj

Warm, دافي dâfi

Wash, v. غسل gasal

Waste, v. اتلف atlaf

Watch, v. سهر sahir

Watch, s. ساعة sâᵉah

Water, ماء * مويه *mâ, mowhy-yah*

Wax, شمع *shame*

Way, طريق *tarî'k*

Wear, v. لبس *labis*

Weave, نسج *nasaj*

Weight, وزن *wazn*

Well (good), طيب *ty-ib*

Wet, مبلول *mablool*

Whisper, وشوش * ناجي *nâja, washwash*

Whole, جملة * تمام *jomlah, tamâm*

Wide, واسع *wâsi*

Wife, زوجة *zoujah*

Wine, شراب * خمر *c'hamr, sharâb*

Wisdom, حكمة *'hikmah*

Wise, حكيم *'hakeem*

Wish, رغبة *ragbah*

Wonderful, عجيب *ajeeb*

Work, عمل *amal*

Workshop, محل العمل *ma-'hall al amal*

Worth, قيمة *'kîmah*

Wound, جرح *jor'h*

Wounded, مجروح *majroo'h*

Wreck (ship), انكسار المركب *inkisâr al marcab*

Write, كتب *catab*

Wrong, خطا * مخطي *'cha'ta, moc'h'ti*

Wrought, معمول *ma mool*

Y.

Yard (measure), ذراع *thirâ*

Year, سنة * عام *sanah, âm*

Yellow, اصفر *a'sfar*

Yesterday, امس * البارحة *ams, al bârî'hah*

Yield, v. (deliver up) سلم *sallam*

Young, شاب*صغير *shâbb, sagîr*

You, انتم *antom*

Youth, شباب *shabâb*

Z.

Zeal, غيرة *geyrah*

Zealous, غيور *ga-yoor*

Zephyr, صبا *'sabâ*

Zero, صفر *'sifr*.